Let's Keep in Touch

Follow Us   Online

Visit US at

www.EffortlessMath.com

 https://www.facebook.com/Effortlessmath

Call

1-469-230-3605

https://goo.gl/2B6qWW

Online Math Lessons

It's easy! Here's how it works.

1- Request a FREE introductory session.

2- Meet a Math tutor online.

3- Start Learning Math in Minutes.

Send Email to: info@EffortlessMath.com

www.learnpersianonline.com

... So Much More Online!

- FREE Farsi lessons

- More Farsi learning books!

- Online Farsi – English Dictionary

- Online Farsi Tutors

Looking for an Online Farsi Tutor?

Send email to: Info@learnpersianonline.com

ISEE UPPER LEVEL Math Workbook 2018

The Most Comprehensive Review for the Math Section of the ISEE UPPER LEVEL TEST

By

Reza Nazari

& Ava Ross

ISEE Upper Level Math Workbook 2018

Copyright © 2018

Reza Nazari & Ava Ross

All rights reserved. No part of this publication may be reproduced, stored in a retrieval system, or transmitted in any form or by any means, electronic, mechanical, photocopying, recording, scanning, or otherwise, except as permitted under Section 107 or 108 of the 1976 United States Copyright Ac, without permission of the author.

All inquiries should be addressed to:

info@effortlessMath.com

www.EffortlessMath.com

ISBN-13: 978-1985587694

ISBN-10: 1985587696

Published by: Effortless Math Education

www.EffortlessMath.com

Description

Effortless Math ISEE UPPER LEVEL Workbook provides students with the confidence and math skills they need to succeed on the ISEE UPPER LEVEL Math, providing a solid foundation of basic Math topics with abundant exercises for each topic. It is designed to address the needs of ISEE UPPER LEVEL test takers who must have a working knowledge of basic Math.

This comprehensive workbook with over 2,500 sample questions and 2 complete ISEE UPPER LEVEL tests is all you need to fully prepare for the ISEE UPPER LEVEL Math. It will help you learn everything you need to ace the math section of the ISEE UPPER LEVEL.

There are more than 2,500 Math problems with answers in this book.

Effortless Math unique study program provides you with an in-depth focus on the math portion of the exam, helping you master the math skills that students find the most troublesome.
This workbook contains most common sample questions that are most likely to appear in the mathematics section of the ISEE UPPER LEVEL.

Inside the pages of this comprehensive Workbook, students can learn basic math operations in a structured manner with a complete study program to help them understand essential math skills. It also has many exciting features, including:

- Dynamic design and easy-to-follow activities
- A fun, interactive and concrete learning process
- Targeted, skill-building practices
- Fun exercises that build confidence
- Math topics are grouped by category, so you can focus on the topics you struggle on
- All solutions for the exercises are included, so you will always find the answers

- 2 Complete ISEE UPPER LEVEL Math Practice Tests that reflect the format and question types on ISEE UPPER LEVEL

Effortless Math ISEE UPPER LEVEL Workbook is an incredibly useful tool for those who want to review all topics being covered on the ISEE UPPER LEVE test. It efficiently and effectively reinforces learning outcomes through engaging questions and repeated practice, helping you to quickly master basic Math skills.

About the Author

Reza Nazari is the author of more than 100 Math learning books including:
– **Math and Critical Thinking Challenges:** For the Middle and High School Student
– **GED Math in 30 Days.**
– **ASVAB Math Workbook 2018 - 2019**
– **Effortless Math Education Workbooks**
– and many more Mathematics books …

Reza is also an experienced Math instructor and a test-prep expert who has been tutoring students since 2008. Reza is the founder of Effortless Math Education, a tutoring company that has helped many students raise their standardized test scores—and attend the colleges of their dreams. Reza provides an individualized custom learning plan and the personalized attention that makes a difference in how students view math.

To ask questions about Math, you can contact Reza via email at:
reza@EffortlessMath.com

Find Reza's professional profile at:
goo.gl/zoC9rJ

Contents

Description 2

CHAPTER 1: Whole Numbers 12

1-1 Place Value 13

1-2 Comparing Numbers 14

1-3 Rounding 15

1-5 Whole Number Multiplication and Division 17

1-6 Rounding and Estimates 18

Answers of Worksheets – Chapter 1 19

Chapter 2: Fractions and Decimals 22

2-1 Simplifying Fractions 23

2-2 Adding and Subtracting Fractions 24

2-3 Multiplying and Dividing Fractions 25

2-4 Adding and Subtracting Mixed Numbers 26

2-5 Multiplying and Dividing Mixed Numbers 27

2-6 Comparing Decimals 28

2-7 Rounding Decimals 29

2-8 Adding and Subtracting Decimals 30

2-9 Multiplying and Dividing Decimals 31

2-10 Converting Between Fractions, Decimals and Mixed Numbers 32

2-11 Divisibility Rules 33

2-12 Factoring Numbers 34

2-13 Greatest Common Factor 35

2-14 Least Common Multiple 36

Answers of Worksheets – Chapter 2 37

Chapter 3: Real Numbers and Integers 44

3-1 Adding and Subtracting Integers 45

3-2 Multiplying and Dividing Integers...46

3-3 Ordering Integers and Numbers 47

3-4 Arrange, Order, and Comparing Integers 48

3-5 Order of Operations...49

3-6 Mixed Integer Computations 50

3-7 Absolute Value...51

3-8 Integers and Absolute Value 52

3-9 Classifying Real Numbers Venn Diagram 53

3-10 Classifying Numbers...54

Answers of Worksheets – Chapter 3..55

Chapter 4: Proportions and Ratios..59

4-1 Writing Ratios 60

4-2 Simplifying Ratios...61

4-3 Proportional Ratios 62

4-4 Create a Proportion 63

4-5 Similar Figures..64

4-6 Similar Figure Word Problems 65

4-7 Simple and Compound Interest 66

4-8 Complete the Ratio Table 67

4-9 Write Each Ratio in Simplest Form 68

4-10 Ratio and Rates Word Problems..69

Answers of Worksheets – Chapter 4..70

Chapter 5: Percent 74

5-1 Converting Between Percents, Fractions, and Decimals 75

5-2 Table of Common Percent 76

5-3 Percentage Calculations...77

5-4 Find What Percentage a Number Is of Another 78

5-5 Find a Percentage of a Given Number 79

5-6 Percent Problems 80

5-7 Percent of Increase and Decrease 81

5-8 Markup, Discount, and Tax 82

Answers of Worksheets – Chapter 5 83

Chapter 6: Algebraic Expressions 87

6-1 Expressions and Variables 88

6-2 Simplifying Variable Expressions 89

6-3 The Distributive Property 90

6-4 Translate Phrases into an Algebraic Statement 91

6-5 Evaluating One Variable 92

6-6 Evaluating Two Variables 93

6-7 Combining like Terms 94

6-8 Simplifying Polynomial Expressions 95

Answers of Worksheets – Chapter 6 96

Chapter 7: Equations 99

7–1 One–Step Equations 100

7–2 One–Step Equation Word Problems 101

7–3 Two–Step Equations 102

7–4 Two–Step Equation Word Problems 103

7–5 Multi–Step Equations 104

Answers of Worksheets – Chapter 7 105

Chapter 8: Systems of Equations 107

8-1 Solving Systems of Equations by Graphing 108

8-2 Solving Systems of Equations by Substitution 109

8-3 Solving Systems of Equations by Elimination 110

8-4 Systems of Equations Word Problems 111

Answers of Worksheets – Chapter 8 112

Chapter 9: Inequalities 114

9-1 Graphing Single-Variable Inequalities 115

9-2 One-Step Inequalities 116

9-3 Two-Step Inequalities 117

9-4 Multi-Step Inequalities 118

Answers of Worksheets – Chapter 8 119

Chapter 10: Linear Functions 122

10-1 Finding Slope 123

10-2 Graphing Lines Using Slope-Intercept Form 124

10-3 Graphing Lines Using Standard Form 125

10-4 Writing Linear Equations 126

10-5 Graphing Linear Inequalities 127

10-6 Finding Midpoint 128

10-7 Finding Distance of Two Points 129

Answers of Worksheets – Chapter 9 130

Chapter 11: Polynomials 136

11-1 Writing Polynomials in Standard Form 137

11-2 Simplifying Polynomials 138

11-3 Adding and Subtracting Polynomials 139

11-4 Multiplying Monomials 140

11-5 Multiplying and Dividing Monomials 141

11-6 Multiplying a Polynomial and a Monomial 142

11-7 Multiplying Binomials 143

11-8 Factoring Trinomials 144

11-9 Operations with Polynomials 145

Answers of Worksheets – Chapter 10 146

Chapter 12: Exponents and Radicals 150

12-1 Multiplication Property of Exponents 151

12-2 Division Property of Exponents 152

12-3 Powers of Products and Quotients 153

12-4 Zero and Negative Exponents 154

12-5 Negative Exponents and Negative Bases 155

12-6 Writing Scientific Notation 156

12-7 Square Roots 157

Answers of Worksheets – Chapter 12 158

Chapter 13: Geometry 161

13-1 The Pythagorean Theorem 162

13-2 Classifying Triangles and Quadrilaterals 163

13-3 Area of Triangles 164

13-4 Perimeter of Polygons 165

13-5 Area and Circumference of Circles 166

13-6 Area of Squares, Rectangles, and Parallelograms 167

13-7 Area of Trapezoids 168

Answers of Worksheets – Chapter 13 169

Chapter 14: Solid Figures 171

14-1 Classifying Solids 172

14-2 Volume of Cubes and Rectangle Prisms 173

14-3 Surface Area of Cubes 174

14-4 Surface Area of a Prism 175

14-5 Surface Area of a Cylinder 176

14-6 Surface Area of Pyramids and Cones 177

14-7 Surface Area of a Sphere 178

14-8 Volume of a Pyramid and Cone 179

14-9 Volume of a Sphere 180

Answers of Worksheets – Chapter 14 181

Chapter 15: Statistics 183

15-1 Mean, Median, Mode, and Range of the Given Data 184

15-2 Bar Graph 185

15-3 Box and Whisker Plots 186

15-4 Stem-And-Leaf Plot 187

15-5 The Pie Graph or Circle Graph 188

15-6 Scatter Plots 189

15-7 Probability Problems 190

Answers of Worksheets – Chapter 15 191

ISEE Upper Level Mathematics Achievement Practice Test 1 196

ISEE Upper Level Mathematics Achievement Practice Test 2 220

ISEE Upper Level Tests Answer Keys 240

CHAPTER 1: Whole Numbers

1-1 Place Value

1-2 Comparing Numbers

1-3 Rounding

1-4 Whole Number Addition and Subtraction

1-5 Whole Number Multiplication and Division

1-6 Rounding and Estimates

1-1 Place Value

Write each number in expanded form.

1) Thirty five   30 + 5

2) Sixty seven   ___ + ___

3) Forty two   ___ + ___

4) Eighty nine   ___ + ___

5) Ninety one   ___ + ___

Circle the correct.

6) The 2 in 72 is in the   ones place   tens place   hundreds place

7) The 6 in 65 is in the   ones place   tens place   hundreds place

8) The 2 in 342 is in the   ones place   tens place   hundreds place

9) The 5 in 450 is in the   ones place   tens place   hundreds place

10) The 3 in 321 is in the   ones place   tens place   hundreds place

1-2 Comparing Numbers

Use > = <.

1) 35 67
2) 89 56
3) 56 35
4) 27 56
5) 34 34
6) 28 45
7) 89 67
8) 90 56
9) 94 98
10) 48 23
11) 24 54
12) 89 89
13) 50 30
14) 20 20

Use less than, equal to or greater than.

1. 23 _____ 34
2. 89 _____ 98
3. 45 _____ 25
4. 34 _____ 32
5. 91 _____ 91
6. 57 _____ 55
7. 85 _____ 78
8. 56 _____ 43
9. 34 _____ 34
10. 92 _____ 98
11. 38 _____ 46
12. 67 _____ 58
13. 88 _____ 69
14. 23 _____ 34

1-3 Rounding

Round each number to the underlined place value.

1) 9̲72

2) 2,9̲95

3) 36̲4

4) 8̲1

5) 5̲5

6) 33̲4

7) 1,2̲03

8) 9.5̲7

9) 7.4̲84

10) 9.1̲4

11) 3̲9

12) 9̲,123

13) 3,45̲2

14) 5̲69

15) 1,2̲30

16) 9̲8

17) 9̲3

18) 3̲7

19) 49̲3

20) 2,9̲23

21) 9̲,845

22) 55̲5

23) 9̲39

24) 6̲9

1-4 Whole Number Addition and Subtraction

1) A school had 891 students last year. If all last year students and 338 new students have registered for this year, how many students will there be in total?

2) Alice has just started her first job after graduating from college. Her yearly income is $33,000 per year. Alice's father income is $56,000 per year and her mother's income is $49,000. What is yearly income of Alice and her parent altogether?

3) Tom had $895 dollars in his saving account. He gave $235 dollars to his sister, Lisa. How much money does he have left?

4) Emily has 830 marbles, Daniel has 970 marbles, and Ethan has 230 marbles less than Daniel. How many marbles do they have in all?

Find the missing number.

5) 890 – .... = 300

6) 1000 – .... = 200

7) .... – 4000 = 92000

8) 60000 – 51000 = ...

9) 3400 – .... = 3200

10) 33000 – 5000 = ...

1-5 Whole Number Multiplication and Division

Multiply and divided.

1) $340 \div 8 =$

2) $1800 \div 20 =$

3) $50000 \div 10 =$

4) $966 \div 30 =$

5) $201 \times 20 =$

6) $400 \times 50 =$

7) $400 \times 90 =$

8) $888 \times 90 =.$

9) $80 \times 80 =$

10) $122 \times 12 =$

11) $609 \times 8 =$

12) $220 \times 12 =$

13) A group of 235 students has collected $8,565 for charity during last month. They decided to split the money evenly among 5 charities. How much will each charity receive?

14) Maria and her two brothers have 9 boxes of crayons. Each box contains 56 crayons. How many crayons do Maria and her two brothers have?

1-6 Rounding and Estimates

Estimate the sum by rounding each added to the nearest ten.

1) 55 + 9

2) 13 + 74

3) 83 + 7

4) 32 + 37

5) 13 + 74

6) 34 + 11

7) 39 + 77

8) 25 + 4

9) 61 + 73

10) 64 + 59

11) 14 + 68

12) 82 + 12

13) 43 + 66

14) 45 + 65

15) 553 + 232

16) 418 + 846

17) 582 + 277

18) 2771 + 1651

19) 7436 + 3575

20) 1542 + 8738

21) 3843 + 6579

22) 4722 + 8186

23) 2419 + 7224

24) 6768 + 3169

Answers of Worksheets – Chapter 1

1-1 Place Value

1) 30 + 5
2) 60 + 7
3) 40 + 2
4) 80 + 9
5) 90 + 1

6) ones place
7) tens place
8) ones place
9) tens place
10) hundreds place

1-2 Comparing Numbers

1) 35 < 67
2) 89 > 56
3) 56 > 35
4) 27 < 56
5) 34 = 34
6) 28 < 45
7) 89 > 67
8) 90 > 56
9) 94 < 98
10) 48 > 23
11) 24 < 54
12) 89 = 89
13) 50 > 30
14) 20 = 20

15) 23 less than 34
16) 89 less than 98
17) 45 greater than 25
18) 34 greater than 32
19) 91 equal to 91
20) 57 greater than 55
21) 85 greater than 78
22) 56 greater than 43
23) 34 equal to 34
24) 92 less than 98
25) 38 less than 46
26) 67 greater than 58
27) 88 greater than 69
28) 23 less than 34

1-3 Rounding

1) 1000
2) 3000
3) 360
4) 70
5) 50
6) 330
7) 1200
8) 9.6
9) 7.5
10) 9.1
11) 40
12) 9000
13) 3,450
14) 600
15) 1,200
16) 100
17) 90
18) 40
19) 490
20) 2,900
21) 10,000
22) 560
23) 900
24) 70

1-4 Whole Number Addition and Subtraction

1) 1229
2) 138000
3) 660
4) 2540
5) 590
6) 800
7) 96000
8) 9000
9) 200
10) 28000

1-5 Whole Number Multiplication and Division

1) 42.5
2) 90
3) 5000
4) 32.2
5) 4020
6) 20000
7) 36000
8) 79920
9) 6400
10) 1464
11) 4872
12) 2640
13) 1713
14) 504

1-6 Rounding and Estimates

1) 70
2) 80
3) 90
4) 70
5) 80
6) 40
7) 120
8) 30
9) 130

10) 120

11) 80

12) 90

13) 110

14) 120

15) 780

16) 1270

17) 860

18) 4420

19) 11020

20) 10280

21) 10420

22) 12910

23) 9640

24) 9940

Chapter 2: Fractions and Decimals

2-1 Simplifying Fractions

2-2 Adding and Subtracting Fractions

2-3 Multiplying and Dividing Fractions

2-4 Adding and Subtracting Mixed Numbers

2-5 Multiplying and Dividing Mixed Numbers

2-6 Comparing Decimals

2-7 Rounding Decimals

2-8 Adding and Subtracting Decimals

2-9 Multiplying and Dividing Decimals

2-10 Converting Between Fractions, Decimals and Mixed Numbers

2-11 Divisibility Rules

2-12 Factoring Numbers

2-13 Greatest Common Factor

2-14 Least Common Multiple

2-1 Simplifying Fractions

Simplify the fractions.

1) $\dfrac{22}{36}$

2) $\dfrac{8}{10}$

3) $\dfrac{12}{18}$

4) $\dfrac{6}{8}$

5) $\dfrac{13}{39}$

6) $\dfrac{5}{20}$

7) $\dfrac{16}{36}$

8) $\dfrac{18}{36}$

9) $\dfrac{20}{50}$

10) $\dfrac{6}{54}$

11) $\dfrac{45}{81}$

12) $\dfrac{21}{28}$

13) $\dfrac{35}{56}$

14) $\dfrac{52}{64}$

15) $\dfrac{13}{65}$

16) $\dfrac{44}{77}$

17) $\dfrac{21}{42}$

18) $\dfrac{15}{36}$

19) $\dfrac{9}{24}$

20) $\dfrac{20}{80}$

21) $\dfrac{25}{45}$

2-2 Adding and Subtracting Fractions

Add fractions.

1) $\frac{2}{3} + \frac{1}{2}$

2) $\frac{3}{5} + \frac{1}{3}$

3) $\frac{5}{6} + \frac{1}{2}$

4) $\frac{7}{4} + \frac{5}{9}$

5) $\frac{2}{5} + \frac{1}{5}$

6) $\frac{3}{7} + \frac{1}{2}$

7) $\frac{3}{4} + \frac{2}{5}$

8) $\frac{2}{3} + \frac{1}{5}$

9) $\frac{16}{25} + \frac{3}{5}$

Subtract fractions.

10) $\frac{4}{5} - \frac{2}{5}$

11) $\frac{3}{5} - \frac{2}{7}$

12) $\frac{1}{2} - \frac{1}{3}$

13) $\frac{8}{9} - \frac{3}{5}$

14) $\frac{3}{7} - \frac{3}{14}$

15) $\frac{4}{15} - \frac{1}{10}$

16) $\frac{3}{4} - \frac{13}{18}$

17) $\frac{5}{8} - \frac{2}{5}$

18) $\frac{1}{2} - \frac{1}{9}$

2-3 Multiplying and Dividing Fractions

Multiplying fractions. Then simplify.

1) $\dfrac{1}{5} \times \dfrac{2}{3}$

2) $\dfrac{3}{4} \times \dfrac{2}{3}$

3) $\dfrac{2}{5} \times \dfrac{3}{7}$

4) $\dfrac{3}{8} \times \dfrac{1}{3}$

5) $\dfrac{3}{5} \times \dfrac{2}{5}$

6) $\dfrac{7}{9} \times \dfrac{1}{3}$

7) $\dfrac{2}{3} \times \dfrac{3}{8}$

8) $\dfrac{1}{4} \times \dfrac{1}{3}$

9) $\dfrac{5}{7} \times \dfrac{7}{12}$

Dividing fractions.

10) $\dfrac{2}{9} \div \dfrac{1}{4}$

11) $\dfrac{1}{2} \div \dfrac{1}{3}$

12) $\dfrac{6}{11} \div \dfrac{3}{4}$

13) $\dfrac{11}{14} \div \dfrac{1}{10}$

14) $\dfrac{3}{5} \div \dfrac{5}{9}$

15) $\dfrac{1}{2} \div \dfrac{1}{2}$

16) $\dfrac{3}{5} \div \dfrac{1}{5}$

17) $\dfrac{12}{21} \div \dfrac{3}{7}$

18) $\dfrac{5}{14} \div \dfrac{9}{10}$

2-4 Adding and Subtracting Mixed Numbers

Add.

1) $4\frac{1}{2} + 5\frac{1}{2}$

2) $2\frac{3}{8} + 3\frac{1}{8}$

3) $5\frac{3}{5} + 5\frac{1}{5}$

4) $1\frac{1}{3} + 2\frac{2}{3}$

5) $5\frac{1}{6} + 5\frac{1}{2}$

6) $3\frac{1}{3} + 1\frac{1}{3}$

7) $1\frac{10}{11} + 1\frac{1}{3}$

8) $2\frac{3}{6} + 1\frac{1}{2}$

9) $5\frac{3}{5} + 5\frac{1}{5}$

10) $7 + \frac{1}{5}$

11) $1\frac{5}{7} + \frac{1}{3}$

12) $2\frac{1}{4} + 1\frac{2}{4}$

Subtract.

1) $4\frac{1}{2} - 3\frac{1}{2}$

2) $3\frac{3}{8} - 3\frac{1}{8}$

3) $6\frac{3}{5} - 5\frac{1}{5}$

4) $2\frac{1}{3} - 1\frac{2}{3}$

5) $6\frac{1}{6} - 5\frac{1}{2}$

6) $3\frac{1}{3} - 1\frac{1}{3}$

7) $2\frac{10}{11} - 1\frac{1}{3}$

8) $2\frac{1}{2} - 1\frac{1}{2}$

9) $6\frac{3}{5} - 2\frac{1}{5}$

10) $7\frac{2}{5} - 1\frac{1}{5}$

11) $2\frac{5}{7} - 1\frac{1}{3}$

12) $2\frac{1}{4} - 1\frac{1}{2}$

2-5 Multiplying and Dividing Mixed Numbers

Find each product.

1) $1\frac{2}{3} \times 1\frac{1}{4}$

2) $1\frac{3}{5} \times 1\frac{2}{3}$

3) $1\frac{2}{3} \times 3\frac{2}{7}$

4) $4\frac{1}{8} \times 1\frac{2}{5}$

5) $2\frac{2}{5} \times 3\frac{1}{5}$

6) $1\frac{1}{3} \times 1\frac{2}{3}$

7) $1\frac{5}{8} \times 2\frac{1}{2}$

8) $3\frac{2}{5} \times 2\frac{1}{5}$

9) $2\frac{2}{3} \times 4\frac{1}{4}$

10) $2\frac{3}{5} \times 1\frac{2}{4}$

11) $1\frac{1}{3} \times 1\frac{1}{4}$

12) $3\frac{2}{5} \times 1\frac{1}{5}$

Find each quotient.

13) $2\frac{1}{5} \div 2\frac{1}{2}$

14) $2\frac{3}{5} \div 1\frac{1}{3}$

15) $3\frac{1}{6} \div 4\frac{2}{3}$

16) $1\frac{2}{3} \div 3\frac{1}{3}$

17) $4\frac{1}{8} \div 2\frac{2}{4}$

18) $3\frac{1}{2} \div 2\frac{3}{5}$

19) $3\frac{5}{9} \div 1\frac{2}{5}$

20) $2\frac{2}{7} \div 1\frac{1}{2}$

21) $3\frac{1}{5} \div 1\frac{1}{2}$

22) $4\frac{3}{5} \div 2\frac{1}{3}$

23) $6\frac{1}{6} \div 1\frac{2}{3}$

24) $2\frac{2}{3} \div 1\frac{1}{3}$

2-6 Comparing Decimals

Write the correct comparison symbol (>, < or =).

1) 1.25   2.3

2) 0.5   0.23

3) 3.2   3.2

4) 4.58   45.8

5) 2.75   0.275

6) 5.2   5

7) 3.1   0.31

8) 6.33   0.733

9) 8   0.8

10) 4.56   0.456

11) 1.12   1.14

12) 2.77   2.78

13) 6.08   6.11

14) 1.11   0.211

15) 2.6   2.55

16) 1.24   1.25

17) 5.52   0.552

18) 0.33   0.033

19) 14.4   14.4

20) 0.05   0.50

21) 0.59   0.7

22) 0.5   0.05

23) 0.90   0.9

24) 0.27   0.4

2-7 Rounding Decimals

Round each decimal number to the nearest place indicated.

1) 0.2_3_

2) 4.0_4_

3) 5._6_23

4) 0.2_6_6

5) _6_.37

6) 0.8_8_

7) 8.2_4_

8) _7_.0760

9) 1.6_2_9

10) 6.3_9_59

11) _1_.9

12) _5_.2167

13) 5._8_63

14) 8.5_4_

15) 80._6_9

16) 6_5_.85

17) 70.7_8_

18) 61_5_.755

19) 1_6_.4

20) 9_5_.81

21) _2_.408

22) 7_6_.3

23) 116.5_1_4

24) 8.0_6_

2-8 Adding and Subtracting Decimals

Add and subtract decimals.

1) 15.14
   -12.18
   $\overline{}$

2) 65.72
   $+43.67$
   $\overline{}$

3) 82.56
   $+12.28$
   $\overline{}$

4) 34.18
   -23.45
   $\overline{}$

5) 90.37
   $+56.97$
   $\overline{}$

6) 45.78
   -23.39
   $\overline{}$

Solve.

7) _____ + 1.3 = 4.8

8) 4.2 + _____ = 11.6

9) 9.9 + _____ = 16

10) 6.9 + _____ = 16.4

11) _____ + 5.1 = 8.6

12) _____ + 7.9 = 15.2

2-9 Multiplying and Dividing Decimals

Find each product.

1) 14.75 × 10.46

2) 7.78 × 9.19

3) 12.56 × 11.65

4) 8.93 × 9.74

5) 15.21 × 12.36

6) 56.19 × 32.43

7) 45.37 × 67.38

8) 98.20 × 100

9) 23.99 × 1000

Find each quotient.

10) 9.2 ÷ 3.6

11) 27.6 ÷ 3.8

12) 12.6 ÷ 4.7

13) 6.5 ÷ 8.1

14) 1. 4 ÷ 10

15) 3.6 ÷ 100

16) 4.24 ÷ 10

17) 14.6 ÷ 100

2-10 Converting Between Fractions, Decimals and Mixed Numbers

Convert fractions to decimals.

1) $\dfrac{9}{10}$

2) $\dfrac{56}{100}$

3) $\dfrac{3}{4}$

4) $\dfrac{2}{5}$

5) $\dfrac{1}{3}$

6) $\dfrac{4}{5}$

7) $\dfrac{5}{6}$

8) $\dfrac{5}{8}$

9) $\dfrac{13}{21}$

Convert decimal into fraction.

10) 0.3

11) 4.5

12) 2.5

13) 2.3

14) 0.8

15) 0.25

16) 0.14

17) 0.2

18) 0.08

19) 0.45

20) 2.6

21) 5.2

2-11 Divisibility Rules

Use the divisibility rules to underline the answers.

8	<u>2</u> 3 <u>4</u> 5 6 7 <u>8</u> 9 10
1) 16	2 3 4 5 6 7 8 9 10
2) 10	2 3 4 5 6 7 8 9 10
3) 15	2 3 4 5 6 7 8 9 10
4) 28	2 3 4 5 6 7 8 9 10
5) 36	2 3 4 5 6 7 8 9 10
6) 15	2 3 4 5 6 7 8 9 10
7) 27	2 3 4 5 6 7 8 9 10
8) 70	2 3 4 5 6 7 8 9 10
9) 57	2 3 4 5 6 7 8 9 10
10) 102	2 3 4 5 6 7 8 9 10
11) 144	2 3 4 5 6 7 8 9 10
12) 75	2 3 4 5 6 7 8 9 10

2-12 Factoring Numbers

List all positive factors of each number.

1) 68
2) 56
3) 24
4) 40
5) 86
6) 78
7) 50
8) 98
9) 45
10) 26
11) 54
12) 28
13) 55
14) 85
15) 50

List the prime factorization for each number.

16) 50
17) 25
18) 69
19) 21
20) 45
21) 68
22) 26
23) 86
24) 93

2-13 Greatest Common Factor

Find the GCF for each number pair.

1) 20, 30

2) 4, 14

3) 5, 45

4) 68, 12

5) 5, 12

6) 15, 27

7) 3, 24

8) 34, 6

9) 4, 10

10) 5, 3

11) 6, 16

12) 30, 3

13) 24, 28

14) 70, 10

15) 45, 8

16) 90, 35

17) 78, 34

18) 55, 75

19) 60, 72

20) 100, 78

21) 30, 40

2-14 Least Common Multiple

Find the LCM for each number pair.

1) 4, 14

2) 5, 15

3) 16, 10

4) 4, 34

5) 8, 3

6) 12, 24

7) 9, 18

8) 5, 6

9) 8, 19

10) 9, 21

11) 19, 29

12) 7, 6

13) 25, 6

14) 4, 8

15) 30, 10, 50

16) 18, 36, 27

17) 12, 8, 18

18) 8, 18, 4

19) 26, 20, 30

20) 10, 4, 24

21) 15, 30, 45

Answers of Worksheets – Chapter 2

2–1 Simplifying Fractions

1) $\frac{11}{18}$
2) $\frac{4}{5}$
3) $\frac{2}{3}$
4) $\frac{3}{4}$
5) $\frac{1}{3}$
6) $\frac{1}{4}$
7) $\frac{4}{9}$
8) $\frac{1}{2}$
9) $\frac{2}{5}$
10) $\frac{1}{9}$
11) $\frac{5}{9}$
12) $\frac{3}{4}$
13) $\frac{5}{8}$
14) $\frac{13}{16}$
15) $\frac{1}{5}$
16) $\frac{4}{7}$
17) $\frac{1}{2}$
18) $\frac{5}{12}$
19) $\frac{3}{8}$
20) $\frac{1}{4}$
21) $\frac{5}{9}$

2–2 Adding and Subtracting Fractions

1) $\frac{7}{6}$
2) $\frac{14}{15}$
3) $\frac{4}{3}$
4) $\frac{83}{36}$
5) $\frac{3}{5}$
6) $\frac{13}{14}$
7) $\frac{23}{20}$
8) $\frac{13}{15}$
9) $\frac{31}{25}$
10) $\frac{2}{5}$
11) $\frac{11}{35}$
12) $\frac{1}{6}$
13) $\frac{13}{45}$
14) $\frac{3}{14}$
15) $\frac{1}{6}$
16) $\frac{1}{36}$
17) $\frac{9}{40}$
18) $\frac{7}{18}$

2–3 Multiplying and Dividing Fractions

1) $\dfrac{2}{15}$

2) $\dfrac{1}{2}$

3) $\dfrac{6}{35}$

4) $\dfrac{1}{8}$

5) $\dfrac{6}{25}$

6) $\dfrac{7}{27}$

7) $\dfrac{1}{4}$

8) $\dfrac{1}{12}$

9) $\dfrac{5}{12}$

10) $\dfrac{8}{9}$

11) $\dfrac{3}{2}$

12) $\dfrac{8}{11}$

13) $\dfrac{55}{7}$

14) $\dfrac{27}{25}$

15) 1

16) 3

17) $\dfrac{4}{3}$

18) $\dfrac{25}{63}$

2–4 Adding and Subtracting Mixed Numbers

1) 10

2) $5\dfrac{1}{2}$

3) $10\dfrac{4}{5}$

4) 4

5) $10\dfrac{2}{3}$

6) $4\dfrac{2}{3}$

7) $3\dfrac{8}{33}$

8) 4

9) $10\dfrac{4}{5}$

10) $7\dfrac{1}{5}$

11) $2\dfrac{1}{21}$

12) $3\dfrac{3}{4}$

13) 1

14) $\dfrac{1}{4}$

15) $1\dfrac{2}{5}$

16) $\dfrac{2}{3}$

17) $\dfrac{2}{3}$

18) 2

19) $1\dfrac{19}{33}$

20) 1

21) $4\dfrac{2}{5}$

22) $6\dfrac{1}{5}$

23) $1\dfrac{8}{21}$

24) $\dfrac{3}{4}$

2–5 Multiplying and Dividing Mixed Numbers

1) $2\frac{1}{12}$
2) $2\frac{2}{3}$
3) $5\frac{10}{21}$
4) $5\frac{31}{40}$
5) $7\frac{17}{25}$
6) $2\frac{2}{9}$
7) $4\frac{1}{16}$
8) $7\frac{12}{25}$
9) $11\frac{1}{3}$
10) $3\frac{9}{10}$
11) $1\frac{2}{3}$
12) $4\frac{2}{25}$
13) $\frac{22}{25}$
14) $1\frac{19}{20}$
15) $\frac{19}{28}$
16) $\frac{1}{2}$
17) $1\frac{13}{20}$
18) $1\frac{9}{26}$
19) $2\frac{34}{63}$
20) $1\frac{11}{20}$
21) $2\frac{2}{15}$
22) $1\frac{34}{35}$
23) $3\frac{7}{10}$
24) 2

2-6 Comparing Decimals

1) 1.25 < 2.3
2) 0.5 > 0.23
3) 3.2 = 3.2
4) 4.58 < 45.8
5) 2.75 > 0.275
6) 5.2 > 5
7) 3.1 > 0.31
8) 6.33 > 0.733
9) 8 > 0.8
10) 4.56 > 0.456
11) 1.12 < 1.14
12) 2.77 < 2.78
13) 6.08 < 6.11
14) 1.11 > 0.211
15) 2.6 > 2.55
16) 1.24 < 1.25
17) 5.52 > 0.552
18) 0.33 > 0.033
19) 14.4 = 14.4
20) 0.05 < 0.50
21) 0.59 < 0.7
22) 0.3 > 0.03
23) 0.90 = 0.9
24) 0.27 < 0.4

2-7 Rounding Decimals

1) 0.2
2) 4.0
3) 5.6
4) 0.3
5) 6
6) 0.9
7) 8.2
8) 7
9) 1.63
10) 6.4
11) 2
12) 5
13) 5.9
14) 8.5
15) 81

16) 66	19) 16	22) 76
17) 70.8	20) 96	23) 116.5
18) 616	21) 2	24) 8.1

2–8 Adding and Subtracting Decimals

1) 2.96	5) 147.34	9) 6.1
2) 109.39	6) 22.39	10) 9.5
3) 94.84	7) 3.5	11) 3.5
4) 10.73	8) 7.4	12) 7.3

2–9 Multiplying and Dividing Decimals

1) 7.2	7) 44.46	13) 0.8024…
2) 76.23	8) 9820	14) 0.14
3) 3.9	9) 23990	15) 0.036
4) 86.33	10) 2.5555…	16) 0.424
5) 190.26	11) 7.2631…	17) 0.146
6) 22.77	12) 2.6808…	

2–10 Converting Between Fractions, Decimals and Mixed Numbers

1) 0.9	10) $\frac{3}{10}$	16) $\frac{7}{50}$
2) 0.56	11) $4\frac{1}{2}$	17) $\frac{1}{5}$
3) 0.75	12) $2\frac{1}{2}$	18) $\frac{2}{25}$
4) 0.4	13) $2\frac{3}{10}$	19) $\frac{9}{20}$
5) 0.333…	14) $\frac{4}{5}$	20) $2\frac{3}{5}$
6) 0.8	15) $\frac{1}{4}$	21) $5\frac{1}{5}$
7) 0.8333…		
8) 0.625		
9) 0.6190…		

2-11 Divisibility Rules

8	<u>2</u> 3 <u>4</u> 5 6 7 <u>8</u> 9 10
1) 16	<u>2</u> 3 <u>4</u> 5 6 7 <u>8</u> 9 10
2) 10	<u>2</u> 3 4 <u>5</u> 6 7 8 9 <u>10</u>
3) 15	2 <u>3</u> 4 <u>5</u> 6 7 8 9 10
4) 28	<u>2</u> 3 <u>4</u> 5 6 <u>7</u> 8 9 10
5) 36	<u>2</u> <u>3</u> <u>4</u> 5 <u>6</u> 7 8 <u>9</u> 10
6) 18	<u>2</u> <u>3</u> 4 5 <u>6</u> 7 8 <u>9</u> 10
7) 27	2 <u>3</u> 4 5 6 7 8 <u>9</u> 10
8) 70	<u>2</u> 3 4 <u>5</u> 6 <u>7</u> 8 9 <u>10</u>
9) 57	2 <u>3</u> 4 5 6 7 8 9 10
10) 102	<u>2</u> <u>3</u> 4 5 <u>6</u> 7 8 9 10
11) 144	<u>2</u> <u>3</u> <u>4</u> 5 <u>6</u> 7 <u>8</u> <u>9</u> 10
12) 75	2 <u>3</u> 4 <u>5</u> 6 7 8 9 10

2–12 Factoring Numbers

1) 1, 2, 4, 17, 34, 68
2) 1, 2, 4, 7, 8, 14, 28, 56
3) 1, 2, 3, 4, 6, 8, 12, 24
4) 1, 2, 4, 5, 8, 10, 20, 40
5) 1, 2, 43, 86
6) 1, 2, 3, 6, 13, 26, 39, 78
7) 1, 2, 5, 10, 25, 50
8) 1, 2, 7, 14, 49, 98
9) 1, 3, 5, 9, 15, 45
10) 1, 2, 13, 26
11) 1, 2, 3, 6, 9, 18, 27, 54
12) 1, 2, 4, 7, 14, 28
13) 1, 5, 11, 55
14) 1, 5, 17, 85
15) 1, 2, 5, 10, 25, 50
16) $2 \times 5 \times 5$
17) 5×5
18) 3×23
19) 3×7
20) $3 \times 3 \times 5$
21) $2 \times 2 \times 17$
22) 2×13
23) 2×43
24) 3×31

2–13 Greatest Common Factor

1) 10
2) 2
3) 5
4) 4
5) 1
6) 3
7) 3
8) 2
9) 2
10) 1
11) 2
12) 3
13) 4
14) 10
15) 1
16) 5
17) 2
18) 5
19) 12
20) 2
21) 10

2–14 Least Common Multiple

1) 28
2) 15
3) 80
4) 68
5) 24
6) 24
7) 18
8) 30
9) 152
10) 63
11) 551
12) 42
13) 150
14) 8
15) 150
16) 108
17) 72
18) 72
19) 780
20) 120
21) 90

Chapter 3: Real Numbers and Integers

3-1 Adding and Subtracting Integers

3-2 Multiplying and Dividing Integers

3-3 Ordering Integers and Numbers

3-4 Arrange and Order, Comparing Integers

3-5 Order of Operations

3-6 Mixed Integer Computations

3-7 Absolute Value

3-8 Integers and Absolute Value

3-9 Classifying Real Numbers Venn Diagram

3-10 Real Number Chart

3-1 Adding and Subtracting Integers

Find the sum.

1) $(-12) + (-4)$

2) $5 + (-24)$

3) $(-14) + 23$

4) $(-8) + (39)$

5) $43 + (-12)$

6) $(-23) + (-4) + 3$

7) $4 + (-12) + (-10) + (-25)$

8) $19 + (-15) + 25 + 11$

9) $(-9) + (-12) + (32 - 14)$

10) $4 + (-30) + (45 - 34)$

Find the difference.

11) $(-14) - (-9) - (18)$

12) $(-9) - (-25)$

13) $(-12) - (8)$

14) $(28) - (-4)$

15) $(34) - (2)$

16) $(55) - (-5) + (-4)$

17) $(9) - (2) - (-5)$

18) $(2) - (4) - (-15)$

19) $(23) - (4) - (-34)$

20) $(-45) - (-87)$

3-2 Multiplying and Dividing Integers

Find each product.

1) $(-8) \times (-2)$

2) 3×6

3) $(-4) \times 5 \times (-6)$

4) $2 \times (-6) \times (-6)$

5) $11 \times (-12)$

6) $10 \times (-5)$

7) 8×8

8) $(-8) \times (-9)$

9) $6 \times (-5) \times 3$

10) $6 \times (-1) \times 2$

Find each quotient.

11) $18 \div 3$

12) $(-24) \div 4$

13) $(-63) \div (-9)$

14) $54 \div 9$

15) $20 \div (-2)$

16) $(-66) \div (-11)$

17) $64 \div 8$

18) $(-121) \div 11$

19) $72 \div 9$

20) $16 \div 4$

3-3 Ordering Integers and Numbers

Order each set of integers from least to greatest.

1) $-15, -19, 20, -4, 1$ ___, ___, ___, ___, ___

2) $6, -5, 4, -3, 2$ ___, ___, ___, ___, ___

3) $15, -42, 19, 0, -22$ ___, ___, ___, ___, ___

4) $26, -91, 0, -13, 67, -55$ ___, ___, ___, ___, ___

5) $-17, -71, 90, -25, -54, -39$ ___, ___, ___, ___, ___, ___

6) $98, 5, 46, 19, 77, 24$ ___, ___, ___, ___, ___, ___

Order each set of integers from greatest to least.

7) $-2, 5, -3, 6, -4$ ___, ___, ___, ___, ___

8) $-37, 7, -17, 27, 47$ ___, ___, ___, ___, ___

9) $32, -27, 19, -17, 15$ ___, ___, ___, ___, ___

10) $68, 81, 21, -18, 94, 72$ ___, ___, ___, ___, ___, ___

3-4 Arrange, Order, and Comparing Integers

Arrange these integers in descending order.

1) 21, 71, − 18, − 10, 82   ___, ___, ___, ___, ___, ___

2) 15, 11, 20, 12, − 9, − 5   ___, ___, ___, ___, ___, ___

3) − 5, 20, 15, 9, −11   ___, ___, ___, ___, ___, ___

4) 19, 18, − 9, − 6, − 11   ___, ___, ___, ___, ___, ___

5) 56, − 34, − 12, − 5, 32   ___, ___, ___, ___, ___, ___

Compare. Use >, =, <

6) − 8 ___ 12   11) − 56 ___ − 58

7) − 10 ___ −16   12) 78 ___ 87

8) 43 ___ 34   13) − 92 ___ − 102

9) 15 ___ −16   14) − 12 ___ − 12

10) − 354 ___ −345   15) − 721 ___ − 821

3-5 Order of Operations

Evaluate each expression.

1) $(2 \times 2) + 5$

2) $24 - (3 \times 3)$

3) $(6 \times 4) + 8$

4) $25 - (4 \times 2)$

5) $(6 \times 5) + 3$

6) $64 - (2 \times 4)$

7) $25 + (1 \times 8)$

8) $(6 \times 7) + 7$

9) $48 \div (4 + 4)$

10) $(7 + 11) \div (-2)$

11) $9 + (2 \times 5) + 10$

12) $(5 + 8) \times \dfrac{3}{5} + 2$

13) $2 \times 7 - \dfrac{10}{9 - 4}$

14) $(12 + 2 - 5) \times 7 - 1$

15) $\dfrac{7}{5 - 1} \times (2 + 6) \times 2$

16) $20 \div (4 - (10 - 8))$

17) $\dfrac{50}{4\,(5 - 4) - 3}$

18) $2 + (8 \times 2)$

3-6 Mixed Integer Computations

Compute.

1) $(-70) \div (-5)$

2) $(-14) \times 3$

3) $(-4) \times (-15)$

4) $(-65) \div 5$

5) $18 \times (-7)$

6) $(-12) \times (-2)$

7) $\dfrac{(-60)}{(-20)}$

8) $24 \div (-8)$

9) $22 \div (-11)$

10) $\dfrac{(-27)}{3}$

11) $4 \times (-4)$

12) $\dfrac{(-48)}{12}$

13) $(-14) \times (-2)$

14) $(-7) \times (7)$

15) $\dfrac{-30}{-6}$

16) $(-54) \div 6$

17) $(-60) \div (-5)$

18) $(-7) \times (-12)$

19) $(-14) \times 5$

20) $88 \div (-8)$

3-7 Absolute Value

Evaluate.

1) $|-4| + |-12| - 7$

2) $|-5| + |-13|$

3) $-18 + |-5 + 3| - 8$

4) $|27| \div |9|$

5) $|-9| \div |-1|$

6) $|200| \div |-100|$

7) $|55| \div |11|$

8) $|36| \div |-6|$

9) $|25| \times |-5|$

10) $|-3| \times |-8|$

11) $|12| \times |-5|$

12) $|11| \times |-6|$

13) $|-8| \times |4|$

14) $|-9| \times |-7|$

15) $|43 - 67 + 9| + |-11| - 1$

16) $|-45 + 78| + |23| - |45|$

17) $75 + |-11 - 30| - |2|$

18) $|-3 + 15| + |9 + 4| - 1$

3-8 Integers and Absolute Value

Write absolute value of each number.

1) -4

2) -7

3) -8

4) 4

5) 5

6) -10

7) 1

8) 6

9) 8

10) -2

11) -1

12) 10

13) 3

14) 7

15) -5

16) -3

17) -9

18) 2

19) 4

20) -6

21) 9

Evaluate.

22) $|-43| - |12| + 10$

23) $76 + |-15 - 45| - |3|$

24) $30 + |-62| - 46$

25) $|32| - |-78| + 90$

26) $|-35 + 4| + 6 - 4$

27) $|-4| + |-11|$

28) $|-6 + 3 - 4| + |7 + 7|$

29) $|-9| + |-19| - 5$

3-9 Classifying Real Numbers Venn Diagram

Identify all of the subsets of real number system to which each number belongs:

Example:

0.1259 : Rational number

$\sqrt{2}$: Irrational number

3 : Natural number, whole number, Integer, rational number

1) 0

2) -5

3) -8.5

4) $\sqrt{4}$

5) -10

6) 18

7) 6

8) π

9) $1\frac{2}{7}$

10) -1

11) $\sqrt{5}$

3-10 Classifying Numbers

Classify the each number as rational or irrational.

1) $\sqrt{4}$

2) 0.123123123

3) 0.347823

4) $\frac{2}{3}$

5) -4π

6) 1,243,256

7) -810

8) $\sqrt{49}$

9) How are the types of numbers related?

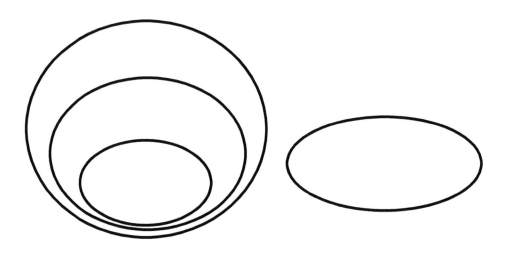

Answers of Worksheets – Chapter 3

3–1 Adding and Subtracting Integers

1) -16	8) 40	15) 32
2) -19	9) -3	16) 56
3) 9	10) -15	17) 12
4) 31	11) -23	18) 13
5) 31	12) 16	19) 53
6) -24	13) -20	20) 42
7) -43	14) 32	

3–2 Multiplying and Dividing Integers

1) 16	8) 72	15) -10
2) 18	9) -90	16) 6
3) 120	10) -12	17) 8
4) 72	11) 6	18) -11
5) -132	12) -6	19) 8
6) -50	13) 7	20) 4
7) 64	14) 6	

3–3 Ordering Integers and Numbers

1) $-19, -15, -4, 1, 20$
2) $-5, -3, 2, 4, 6$
3) $-42, -22, 0, 15, 19$
4) $-91, -55, -13, 0, 26, 67$
5) $-71, -54, -39, -25, -17, 90$
6) $5, 19, 24, 46, 77, 98$
7) $6, 5, -2, -3, -4$
8) $47, 27, 7, -17, -37$
9) $32, 19, 15, -17, -27$
10) $94, 81, 72, 68, 21, -18$

3–4 Arrange and Order, Comparing Integers

1) 82, 71, 21, − 10, − 18
2) 20, 15, 12, 11, − 5, − 9
3) 20, 15, 9, − 5, −11
4) 19, 18, − 6, − 9, − 11
5) 56, 32, − 5, − 12, − 34

6) <   10) <   14) =
7) >   11) >   15) >
8) >   12) <
9) >   13) >

3–5 Order of Operations

1) 9   7) 33   13) 12
2) 15   8) 49   14) 62
3) 32   9) 6   15) 28
4) 17   10) − 9   16) 10
5) 33   11) 29   17) 50
6) 56   12) 9.8   18) 18

3–6 Mixed Integer Computations

1) 14   8) − 3   15) 5
2) − 42   9) − 2   16) − 9
3) 60   10) − 9   17) 12
4) − 13   11) − 16   18) 84
5) − 126   12) − 4   19) − 70
6) 24   13) 28   20) − 11
7) 3   14) − 49

ISEE Upper Level Math Workbook 2018

3–7 Absolute Value

1) 9
2) 18
3) −24
4) 3
5) 9
6) 2
7) 5
8) 6
9) 125
10) 24
11) 60
12) 66
13) 32
14) 63
15) 25
16) 11
17) 114
18) 24

3–8 Integers and Absolute Value

1) 4
2) 7
3) 8
4) 4
5) 5
6) 10
7) 1
8) 6
9) 8
10) 2
11) 1
12) 10
13) 3
14) 7
15) 5
16) 3
17) 9
18) 2
19) 4
20) 6
21) 9
22) 41
23) 133
24) 46
25) 44
26) 33
27) 15
28) 21
29) 23

3–9 Classifying Real Numbers Venn Diagram

1) 0: whole number, integer, rational number
2) -5: integer, rational number
3) −8.5: rational number
4) $\sqrt{4}$: natural number, whole number, integer, rational number
5) −10: integer, rational number
6) 18 : natural number, whole number, integer, rational number
7) 6: natural number, whole number, integer, rational number
8) π: irrational number
9) $1\frac{2}{7}$: rational number

10) − 1: integer, rational number

11) $\sqrt{5}$: irrational number

3-10 Real Number Chart

1) Rational number
2) Irrational number
3) Rational number
4) Irrational number
5) Whole numbers
6) Integers
7) Rational number

8) How are the types of numbers related?

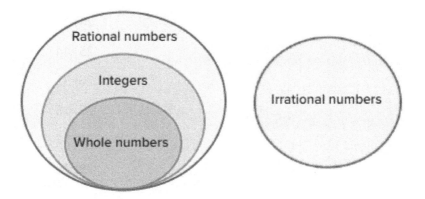

Chapter 4: Proportions and Ratios

4-1 Writing Ratios

4-2 Simplifying Ratios

4-3 Proportional Ratios

4-4 Create a Proportion

4-5 Similar Figures

4-6 Similar Figure Word Problems

4-7 Simple and Compound Interest

4-8 Complete the Ratio Table

4-9 Write Each Ratio in Simplest Form

4-10 Ratio and Rates Word Problems

4-1 Writing Ratios

Express each ratio as a rate and unite rate.

1) 12 miles on 4 gallons of gas.

2) 24 dollars for 6 books.

3) 200 miles on 14 gallons of gas

4) 24 inches of snow in 8 hours

Express each ratio as a fraction in the simplest form.

5) 3 feet out of 30 feet

6) 18 cakes out of 42 cakes

7) 16 dimes t0 24 dimes

8) 12 dimes out of 48 coins

9) 14 cups to 84 cups

10) 45 gallons to 65 gallons

11) 10 miles out of 40 miles

12) 22 blue cars out of 55 cars

13) 32 pennies to 300 pennies

14) 24 beetles out of 86 insects

4-2 Simplifying Ratios

Reduce each ratio.

1) 21 : 49

2) 20 : 40

3) 10 : 50

4) 14 : 18

5) 45 : 27

6) 49 : 21

7) 100 : 10

8) 12 : 8

9) 35 : 45

10) 8 : 20

11) 25 : 35

12) 21 : 27

13) 52 : 82

14) 12 : 36

15) 24 : 3

16) 15 : 30

17) 3 : 36

18) 8 : 16

19) 6 : 100

20) 2 : 20

21) 10 : 60

22) 14 : 63

23) 68 : 80

24) 8 : 80

4-3 Proportional Ratios

Solve each proportion.

1) $\dfrac{3}{6} = \dfrac{8}{d}$

2) $\dfrac{k}{5} = \dfrac{12}{15}$

3) $\dfrac{30}{5} = \dfrac{12}{x}$

4) $\dfrac{x}{2} = \dfrac{1}{8}$

5) $\dfrac{d}{3} = \dfrac{2}{6}$

6) $\dfrac{27}{7} = \dfrac{30}{x}$

7) $\dfrac{8}{5} = \dfrac{k}{15}$

8) $\dfrac{60}{20} = \dfrac{3}{d}$

9) $\dfrac{x}{3} = \dfrac{12}{18}$

10) $\dfrac{25}{5} = \dfrac{x}{8}$

11) $\dfrac{12}{x} = \dfrac{4}{2}$

12) $\dfrac{x}{4} = \dfrac{18}{2}$

13) $\dfrac{80}{10} = \dfrac{k}{10}$

14) $\dfrac{12}{6} = \dfrac{6}{d}$

15) $\dfrac{x}{4} = \dfrac{30}{5}$

16) $\dfrac{9}{5} = \dfrac{k}{5}$

17) $\dfrac{45}{15} = \dfrac{15}{d}$

18) $\dfrac{60}{x} = \dfrac{10}{3}$

19) $\dfrac{d}{3} = \dfrac{14}{6}$

20) $\dfrac{k}{4} = \dfrac{4}{2}$

21) $\dfrac{4}{2} = \dfrac{x}{7}$

4-4 Create a Proportion

Create proportion from the given set of numbers.

1) 1, 6, 2, 3

2) 12, 144, 1, 12

3) 16, 4, 8, 2

4) 9, 5, 27, 15

5) 7, 10, 60, 42

6) 8, 7, 24, 21

7) 10, 5, 8, 4

8) 3, 12, 8, 2

9) 2, 2, 1, 4

10) 3, 6, 7, 14

11) 2, 6, 5, 15

12) 7, 2, 14, 4

4-5 Similar Figures

Each pair of figures is similar. Find the value of x.

1)

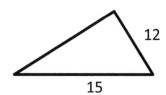

2)

3)

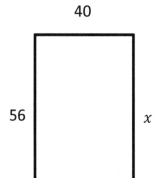

4-6 Similar Figure Word Problems

Answer each question and round your answer to the nearest whole number.

1) If a 42.9 ft tall flagpole casts a 253.1 ft long shadow, then how long is the shadow that a 6.2 ft tall woman casts?

2) A model igloo has a scale of 1 in : 2 ft. If the real igloo is 10 ft wide, then how wide is the model igloo?

3) If a 18 ft tall tree casts a 9 ft long shadow, then how tall is an adult giraffe that casts a 7 ft shadow?

4) Find the distance between San Joe and Mount Pleasant if they are 2 cm apart on a map with a scale of 1 cm : 9 km.

5) A telephone booth that is 8 ft tall casts a shadow that is 4 ft long. Find the height of a lawn ornament that casts a 2 ft shadow.

4-7 Simple and Compound Interest

Use simple interest to find the ending balance.

1) $ 1,300 at 5% for 6 years

2) $ 5,400 at 7.5% for $\frac{1}{2}$

3) $ 25,600 at 9.2% for 5 years

4) $ 24,000 at 8.5% for 9 years

5) $ 450 at 7% for 8 years.

6) $ 54,200 at 8% for 5 years

7) $ 240 interest is earned on a principal of $ 1500 at a simple interest rate of 4% pa. For how many years was the principal invested?

8) A new car, valued at $ 28,000, depreciates at 9% per year. Find the value of the car 3 years after purchase.

9) Joe bought a car for $ 12,400 on the following terms: 15% deposit, 18% simple interest, repayments made monthly for 2 years. How much was the deposit?

4-8 Complete the Ratio Table

Complete the ratio tables.

1)

6		18	
7	14		28

2)

3		9	12
7	14		

3)

10		30	40
5	10		20

4)

1	4	5	9
2			

5)

8		40	48
5	10	25	30

6)

2	4	8	10
3			

7)

11		33	44
15	30		

8)

2	6	8	10
5			

9)

8		40	48
5	10	25	30

10)

3	9	21	27
			36

4-9 Write Each Ratio in Simplest Form

Simplify the ratios below.

1) 4 : 8

2) 3 : 9

3) 8 : 24

4) 3 : 21

5) 12 : 6

6) 4 : 16

7) 4 : 22

8) 12 : 8

9) 24 : 16

10) 25 : 50

11) 40 : 5

12) 3 : 15

13) 9 : 6

14) 18 : 9

15) 6 : 36

16) 28 : 6

17) 14 : 28

18) 3 : 12

19) 8 : 16

20) 49 : 7

21) 110 : 50

4-10 Ratio and Rates Word Problems

Solve.

1) In a party, 10 soft drinks are required for every 12 guests. If there are 252 guests, how many soft drink is required?

2) In Jack's class, 18 of the students are tall and 10 are short. In Michael's class 54 students are tall and 30 students are short. Which class has a higher ratio of tall to short students?

3) Are these ratios equivalent?

   12 cards to 72 animals, 11 marbles to 66 marbles

4) The price of 3 apples at the Quick Market is $1.44. The price of 5 of the same apples at Walmart is $2.50. Which place is the better buy?

5) The bakers at a Bakery can make 160 bagels in 4 hours. How many bagels can they bake in 16 hours? What is that rate per hour?

6) You can buy 5 cans of green beans at a supermarket for $3.40. How much does it cost to buy 35 cans of green beans?

Answers of Worksheets – Chapter 4

4–1 Writing Ratios

1) $\frac{120\ miles}{4\ gallons}$, 30 miles per gallon

2) $\frac{36\ dollars}{6\ books}$, 6.00 dollars per book

3) $\frac{200\ miles}{14\ gallons}$, 14.29 miles per gallon

4) $\frac{24"\ of\ snow}{8\ hours}$, 4.83 inches of snow per hour

5) $\frac{1}{10}$

6) $\frac{3}{7}$

7) $\frac{2}{3}$

8) $\frac{1}{4}$

9) $\frac{1}{6}$

10) $\frac{9}{13}$

11) $\frac{1}{4}$

12) $\frac{2}{5}$

13) $\frac{8}{75}$

14) $\frac{12}{43}$

4–2 Simplifying Ratios

1) 3 : 7
2) 1 : 2
3) 1 : 5
4) 7 : 9
5) 5 : 3
6) 7 : 3
7) 10 : 1
8) 3 : 2
9) 7 : 9
10) 2 : 5
11) 5 : 7
12) 7 : 9
13) 26 : 41
14) 1 : 3
15) 8 : 1
16) 1 : 2
17) 1 : 12
18) 1 : 2
19) 3 : 50
20) 1 : 10
21) 1 : 6
22) 2 : 9
23) 17 : 20
24) 1 : 10

4–3 Proportional Ratios

1) 16	8) 1	15) 24
2) 4	9) 2	16) 9
3) 2	10) 40	17) 5
4) 0.25	11) 6	18) 18
5) 1	12) 36	19) 7
6) 7.78	13) 80	20) 8
7) 24	14) 3	21) 14

4–4 Create a Proportion

1) $1 : 3 = 2 : 6$
2) $12 : 144 = 1 : 12$
3) $2 : 4 = 8 : 16$
4) $5 : 15 = 9 : 27$
5) $7 : 42, 10 : 60$
6) $7 : 21 = 8 : 24$
7) $8 : 10 = 4 : 5$
8) $2 : 3 = 8 : 12$
9) $4 : 2 = 2 : 1$
10) $7 : 3 = 14 : 6$
11) $5 : 2 = 15 : 6$
12) $7 : 2 = 14 : 4$
13) $6 : 7 = 24 : 28$

4–5 Similar Figures

1) 5
2) 3
3) 56

4–6 Similar Figure Word Problems

1) 36.6 ft
2) 5 in
3) 14 ft
4) 18 km
5) 4 ft

4–7 Simple and Compound Interest

1) $ 1,690.00
2) $ 2,902.5
3) $ 37,376.00
4) $ 42,360.00
5) $ 702.00
6) $ 75,880.00
7) 4 years
8) $ 21599.99

9) $ 1860

4–8 Complete the Ratio Table

1)

6	12	18	24
7	14	21	28

2)

3	6	9	12
7	14	21	28

3)

10	20	30	40
5	10	15	20

4)

1	4	5	9
2	8	10	18

5)

8	16	40	48
5	10	25	30

6)

2	4	8	10
3	6	12	15

7)

11	22	33	44
15	30	45	60

8)

2	6	8	10
5	15	20	25

9)

8	16	40	48
5	10	25	30

10)

3	9	21	27
4	12	28	36

4-9 Write Each Ratio in Simplest Form

1) 1 : 2
2) 1 : 3
3) 1 : 3
4) 1 : 7
5) 2 : 1
6) 1 : 4
7) 2 : 11
8) 3 : 2
9) 3 : 2
10) 1 : 2
11) 8 : 1
12) 1 : 5

13) 3 : 2   16) 14 : 3   19) 1 : 2
14) 2 : 1   17) 1 : 2   20) 7 : 1
15) 1 : 6   18) 1 : 4   21) 11 : 5

4–10 Ratio and Rates Word Problems

1) 210

2) The ratio for both class is equal to 9 to 5.

3) Yes! Both ratios are 1 to 6.

4) The price at the Quick Market is a better buy.

5) 640, the rate is 40 per hour.

6) $23.80

Chapter 5: Percent

5-1 Converting Between Percent, Fractions, and Decimals

5-2 Table of Common Percent

5-3 Percentage Calculations

5-4 Find What Percentage a Number Is of Another

5-5 Find a Percentage of a Given Number

5-6 Percent Problems

5-7 Percent of Increase and Decrease

5-8 Markup, Discount, and Tax

5-1 Converting Between Percents, Fractions, and Decimals

Converting fractions to decimals.

1) $\dfrac{50}{100}$

2) $\dfrac{38}{100}$

3) $\dfrac{15}{100}$

4) $\dfrac{80}{100}$

5) $\dfrac{7}{100}$

6) $\dfrac{35}{100}$

7) $\dfrac{90}{100}$

8) $\dfrac{20}{100}$

9) $\dfrac{7}{100}$

Write each decimal as a percent.

10) 0.5

11) 0.9

12) 0.002

13) 0.524

14) 0.1

15) 0.03

16) 3.63

17) 0.008

18) 4.78

5-2 Table of Common Percent

Complete the table of common percent.

Fraction	Decimal	Percent
$\dfrac{1}{25}$	0.04	4%
$\dfrac{1}{2}$		50%
$\dfrac{1}{4}$	0.25	25%
$\dfrac{1}{5}$		20%
$\dfrac{6}{10}$	0.6	
$\dfrac{5}{8}$		62.5 %
$\dfrac{2}{5}$		40%
$\dfrac{7}{100}$	0.07	7%
$\dfrac{7}{16}$		43.75%
$\dfrac{5}{8}$		$62\dfrac{1}{2}\%$
$\dfrac{7}{10}$	0.7	
$\dfrac{30}{100}$		30%
$\dfrac{4}{8}$	0.8	
$\dfrac{3}{4}$		75%

5-3 Percentage Calculations

Calculate the percentages.

1) 50% of 25

2) 80% of 15

3) 30% of 34

4) 70% of 45

5) 10% of 0

6) 80% of 22

7) 65% of 8

8) 78% of 54

9) 50% of 80

10) 20% of 10

11) 40% of 40

12) 90% of 0

13) 20% of 70

14) 55% of 60

15) 80% of 10

16) 20% of 880

17) 70% of 100

18) 80% of 90

Solve.

19) 50 is what percentage of 75?

20) What percentage of 100 is 70

21) Find what percentage of 60 is 35.

22) 40 is what percentage of 80?

5-4 Find What Percentage a Number Is of Another

Find the percentage of the numbers.

1) 45 is what percent of 90?

2) 15 is what percent of 75?

3) 20 is what percent of 400?

4) 18 is what percent of 90?

5) 3 is what percent of 15?

6) 8 is what percent of 80?

7) 11 is what percent of 55?

8) 9 is what percent of 90?

9) 2.5 is what percent of 10?

10) 5 is what percent of 25?

11) 60 is what percent of 20?

12) 12 is what percent of 48?

13) 14 is what percent of 28?

14) 8.2 is what percent of 32.8?

15) 1200 is what percent of 4,800?

16) 4,000 is what percent of 20,000?

17) 45 is what percent of 900?

18) 10 is what percent of 200?

19) 15 is what percent of 60?

20) 1.2 is what percent of 24?

5-5 Find a Percentage of a Given Number

Find a Percentage of a Given Number.

1) 90% of 50

2) 40% of 50

3) 10% of 0

4) 80% of 80

5) 60% of 40

6) 50% of 60

7) 30% of 20

8) 35% of 10

9) 10% of 80

10) 10% of 60

11) 100% 0f 50

12) 90% of 34

13) 80% of 42

14) 90% of 12

15) 20% of 56

16) 40% of 40

17) 40% of 6

18) 70% of 38

19) 30% of 3

20) 40% of 50

21) 100% of 8

5-6 Percent Problems

Solve each problem.

1) 51 is 340% of what?

2) 93% of what number is 97?

3) 27% of 142 is what number?

4) What percent of 125 is 29.3?

5) 60 is what percent of 126?

6) 67 is 67% of what?

7) 67 is 13% of what?

8) 41% of 78 is what?

9) 1 is what percent of 52.6?

10) What is 59% of 14 m?

11) What is 90% of 130 inches?

12) 16 inches is 35% of what?

13) 90% of 54.4 hours is what?

14) What percent of 33.5 is 21?

15) Liam scored 22 out of 30 marks in Algebra, 35 out of 40 marks in science and 89 out of 100 marks in mathematics. In which subject his percentage of marks in best?

16) Ella require 50% to pass her test. If she gets 280 marks and falls short by 20 marks, what were the maximum marks she could have got?

5-7 Percent of Increase and Decrease

Find each percent change to the nearest percent. Increase or Decrease.

1) From 32 grams to 82 grams.

2) From 150 m to 45 m

3) From $438 to $443

4) From 256 ft to 140 ft

5) From 6469 ft to 7488 ft

6) From 36 inches to 90 inches

7) From 54 ft to 104 ft

8) From 84 miles to 24 miles

9) The population of a place in a particular year increased by 15%. Next year it decreased by 15%. Find the net increase or decrease percent in the initial population.

10) The salary of a doctor is increased by 40%. By what percent should the new salary be reduced in order to restore the original salary?

5-8 Markup, Discount, and Tax

Find the selling price of each item.

1) Original price of a microphone: $49.99, discount: 5%, tax: 5%

2) Cost of a pen: $1.95, markup: 70%, discount: 40%, tax: 5%

3) Cost of a puppy: $349.99, markup: 41%, discount: 23%

4) Cost of a shirt: $14.95, markup: 25%, discount: 45%

5) Cost of an oil change: $21.95, markup: 95%

6) Cost of computer: $1,850.00, markup: 75%

Answers of Worksheets – Chapter 5

5–1 Converting Between Percent, Fractions, and Decimals

1) 0.5
2) 0.38
3) 0.15
4) 0.8
5) 0.07
6) 0.35
7) 0.9
8) 0.2
9) 0.07
10) 50%
11) 90%
12) 0.2%
13) 52.4%
14) 10%
15) 3%
16) 363%
17) 0.8%
18) 478%

5–2 Table of Common Percent

Fraction	Decimal	Percent
$\frac{1}{25}$	0.04	4%
$\frac{1}{2}$	0.5	50%
$\frac{1}{4}$	0.25	25%
$\frac{1}{5}$	0.2	20%
$\frac{6}{10}$	0.6	60%
$\frac{5}{8}$	0.625	62.5 %
$\frac{2}{5}$	0.4	40%
$\frac{7}{100}$	0.07	7%

$\frac{7}{16}$	0.4375	43.75%
$\frac{5}{8}$	0.625	625 %
$\frac{7}{10}$	0.7	70%
$\frac{30}{100}$	0.3	30%
$\frac{4}{8}$	0.8	80%
$\frac{3}{4}$	0.75	75%

5–3 Percentage Calculations

1) 12.5
2) 12
3) 10.2
4) 31.5
5) 0
6) 17.6
7) 5.2
8) 42.12
9) 40
10) 2
11) 16
12) 0
13) 14
14) 33
15) 8
16) 176
17) 70
18) 72
19) 67%
20) 70%
21) 58%
22) 50%

5–4 Find What Percentage a Number Is of Another

1) 45 is what percent of 90? 50 %
2) 15 is what percent of 75? 20 %
3) 20 is what percent of 400? 5 %
4) 18 is what percent of 90? 20 %
5) 3 is what percent of 15? 20 %
6) 8 is what percent of 80? 10 %
7) 11 is what percent of 55? 20 %
8) 9 is what percent of 90? 10 %
9) 2.5 is what percent of 10? 25 %
10) 5 is what percent of 25? 20 %

11) 60 is what percent of 20? 300 %

12) 12 is what percent of 48? 25 %

13) 14 is what percent of 28? 50 %

14) 8.2 is what percent of 32.8? 25 %

15) 1200 is what percent of 4,800? 25%

16) 4,000 is what percent of 20,000? 20 %

17) 45 is what percent of 900? 5 %

18) 10 is what percent of 200? 5 %

19) 15 is what percent of 60? 25 %

20) 1.2 is what percent of 24? 5 %

5–5 Find a Percentage of a Given Number

1) 45
2) 20
3) 0
4) 64
5) 24
6) 30
7) 6
8) 3.5
9) 8
10) 6
11) 50
12) 30.6
13) 33.6
14) 10.8
15) 11.2
16) 16
17) 2.4
18) 26.6
19) 0.9
20) 20
21) 8
22)

5-6 Percent Problems

1) 15
2) 104.3
3) 38.34
4) 23.44%
5) 47.6%
6) 100
7) 515.4
8) 31.98
9) 1.9%
10) 8.3 m
11) 117 inches
12) 45.7 inches
13) 49 hours
14) 62.7%
15) Mathematics
16) 600

5–7 Percent of Increase and Decrease

1) 156.25% increase
2) 70% decrease
3) 1.142% increase
4) 45.31% decrease
5) 15.75% increase
6) 92.6% increase
7) 104% increase
8) 71.43% decrease
9) 2.25% decrease
10) $28\frac{4}{7}$

5–8 Markup, Discount, and Tax

1) $49.87
2) $2.09
3) $379.98
4) $10.28
5) $36.22
6) $3,237.50

Chapter 6: Algebraic Expressions

6-1 Expressions and Variables

6-2 Simplifying Variable Expressions

6-3 The Distributive Property

6-4 Translate Phrases into an Algebraic Statement

6-5 Evaluating One Variable

6-6 Evaluating Two Variables

6-7 Combining like Terms

6-8 Simplifying Polynomial Expressions

6-1 Expressions and Variables

Simplify each expression.

1) $x + 5x$,

   use $x = 5$

2) $8(-3x + 9) + 6$,

   use $x = 6$

3) $10x - 2x + 6 - 5$,

   use $x = 5$

4) $2x - 3x - 9$,

   use $x = 7$

5) $(-6)(-2x - 4y)$,

   use $x = 1, y = 3$

6) $8x + 2 + 4y$,

   use $x = 9, y = 2$

7) $(-6)(-8x - 9y)$,

   use $x = 5, y = 5$

8) $6x + 5y$,

   use $x = 7, y = 4$

Simplify each expression.

9) $5(-4 + 2x)$

10) $-3 - 5x - 6x + 9$

11) $6x - 3x - 8 + 10$

12) $(-8)(6x - 4) + 12$

13) $9(7x + 4) + 6x$

14) $(-9)(-5x + 2)$

6-2 Simplifying Variable Expressions

Simplify each expression.

1) $-2 - x^2 - 6x^2$

2) $3 + 10x^2 + 2$

3) $8x^2 + 6x + 7x^2$

4) $5x^2 - 12x^2 + 8x$

5) $2x^2 - 2x - x$

6) $(-6)(8x - 4)$

7) $4x + 6(2 - 5x)$

8) $10x + 8(10x - 6)$

9) $9(-2x - 6) - 5$

10) $3(x + 9)$

11) $7x + 3 - 3x$

12) $2.5x^2 \times (-8x)$

Simplify.

13) $-2(4 - 6x) - 3x$, $x = 1$

14) $2x + 8x$, $x = 2$

15) $9 - 2x + 5x + 2$, $x = 5$

16) $5(3x + 7)$, $x = 3$

17) $2(3 - 2x) - 4$, $x = 6$

18) $5x + 3x - 8$, $x = 3$

19) $x - 7x$, $x = 8$

20) $5(-2 - 9x)$, $x = 4$

6-3 The Distributive Property

Use the distributive property to simply each expression.

1) $-(-2-5x)$

2) $(-6x+2)(-1)$

3) $(-5)(x-2)$

4) $-(7-3x)$

5) $8(8+2x)$

6) $2(12+2x)$

7) $(-6x+8)\,4$

8) $(3-6x)(-7)$

9) $(-12)(2x+1)$

10) $(8-2x)\,9$

11) $(-2x)(-1+9x)-4x(4+5x)$

12) $3(-5x-3)+4(6-3x)$

13) $(-2)(x+4)-(2+3x)$

14) $(-4)(3x-2)+6(x+1)$

15) $(-5)(4x-1)+4(x+2)$

16) $(-3)(x+4)-(2+3x)$

6-4 Translate Phrases into an Algebraic Statement

Write an algebraic expression for each phrase.

1) A number increased by forty–two.

2) The sum of fifteen and a number

3) The difference between fifty–six and a number.

4) The quotient of thirty and a number.

5) Twice a number decreased by 25.

6) Four times the sum of a number and − 12.

7) A number divided by − 20.

8) The quotient of 60 and the product of a number and − 5.

9) Ten subtracted from a number.

10) The difference of six and a number.

6-5 Evaluating One Variable

Simplify each algebraic expression.

1) $9 - x$, $x = 3$

2) $x + 2$, $x = 5$

3) $3x + 7$, $x = 6$

4) $x + (-5)$, $x = -2$

5) $3x + 6$, $x = 4$

6) $4x + 6$, $x = -1$

7) $10 + 2x - 6$, $x = 3$

8) $10 - 3x$, $x = 8$

9) $\frac{20}{x} - 3$, $x = 5$

10) $(-3) + \frac{x}{4} + 2x$, $x = 16$

11) $(-2) + \frac{x}{7}$, $x = 21$

12) $(-\frac{14}{x}) - 9 + 4x$, $x = 2$

13) $(-\frac{6}{x}) - 9 + 2x$, $x = 3$

14) $(-2) + \frac{x}{8}$, $x = 16$

15) $8(5x - 12)$, $x = -2$

6-6 Evaluating Two Variables

Simplify each algebraic expression.

1) $2x + 4y - 3 + 2$,

   $x = 5, y = 3$

2) $(-\frac{12}{x}) + 1 + 5y$,

   $x = 6, y = 8$

3) $(-4)(-2a - 2b)$,

   $a = 5, b = 3$

4) $10 + 3x + 7 - 2y$,

   $x = 7, y = 6$

5) $9x + 2 - 4y$,

   $x = 7, y = 5$

6) $6 + 3(-2x - 3y)$,

   $x = 9, y = 7$

7) $12x + y$,

   $x = 4, y = 8$

8) $x \times 4 \div y$,

   $x = 3, y = 2$

9) $2x + 14 + 4y$,

   $x = 6, y = 8$

10) $4a - (5 - b)$,

    $a = 4, b = 6$

6-7 Combining like Terms

Simplify each expression.

1) $5 + 2x - 8$

2) $(-2x + 6)\,2$

3) $7 + 3x + 6x - 4$

4) $(-4) - (3)(5x + 8)$

5) $9x - 7x - 5$

6) $x - 12x$

7) $7(3x + 6) + 2x$

8) $(-11x) - 10x$

9) $3x - 12 - 5x$

10) $13 + 4x - 5$

11) $(-22x) + 8x$

12) $2(4 + 3x) - 7x$

13) $(-4x) - (6 - 14x)$

14) $5(6x - 1) + 12x$

15) $22x + 6 + 2x$

16) $(-13x) - 14x$

17) $(-6x) - 9 + 15x$

18) $(-6x) + 7x$

19) $(-5x) + 12 + 7x$

20) $(-3x) - 9 + 15x$

21) $20x - 19x$

6-8 Simplifying Polynomial Expressions

Simplify each polynomial.

1) $4x^5 - 5x^6 + 15x^5 - 12x^6 + 3x^6$

2) $(-3x^5 + 12 - 4x) + (8x^4 + 5x + 5x^5)$

3) $10x^2 - 5x^4 + 14x^3 - 20x^4 + 15x^3 - 8x^4$

4) $-6x^2 + 5x^2 - 7x^3 + 12 + 22$

5) $12x^5 - 5x^3 + 8x^2 - 8x^5$

6) $5x^3 + 1 + x^2 - 2x - 10x$

7) $14x^2 - 6x^3 - 2x(4x^2 + 2x)$

8) $(4x^4 - 2x) - (4x - 2x^4)$

9) $(3x^2 + 1) - (4 + 2x^2)$

10) $(2x + 2) - (7x + 6)$

11) $(12x^3 + 4x^4) - (2x^4 - 6x^3)$

12) $(12 + 3x^3) + (6x^3 + 6)$

13) $(5x^2 - 3) + (2x^2 - 3x^3)$

14) $(23x^3 - 12x^2) - (2x^2 - 9x^3)$

15) $(4x - 3x^3) - (3x^3 + 4x)$

Answers of Worksheets – Chapter 6

6–1 Expressions and Variables

1) 30
2) –66
3) 41
4) –16
5) 84
6) 82
7) 510
8) 62
9) 10x – 20
10) 6 – 11x
11) 3x + 2
12) 44 – 48x
13) 69x + 36
14) 45x – 18

6–2 Simplifying Variable Expressions

1) $-7x^2 - 2$
2) $10x^2 + 5$
3) $15x^2 + 6x$
4) $-7x^2 + 8x$
5) $2x^2 - 3x$
6) $-48x + 24$
7) $-26x + 12$
8) 90x – 48
9) –18x – 59
10) 3x + 27
11) 4x + 3
12) $-20x^3$
13) 1
14) 20
15) 26
16) 80
17) –22
18) 16
19) –48
20) –190

6–3 The Distributive Property

1) 5x + 2
2) 6x – 2
3) –5x + 10
4) 3x – 7
5) 16x + 64
6) 4x + 24
7) –24x + 32
8) 42x – 21
9) –24x – 12
10) –18x + 72
11) $-38x^2 - 14x$
12) –27x + 15
13) –5x – 10
14) –6x + 14
15) –16x + 13
16) –6x – 14

6–4 Translate Phrases into an Algebraic Statement

1) x + 42
2) 15 + x
3) 56 − x
4) 30/x
5) 2x − 25
6) 4(x + (−12))
7) $\frac{x}{-20}$
8) $\frac{60}{-5x}$
9) x − 10
10) 6 − x

6–5 Evaluating One Variable

1) 6
2) 7
3) 25
4) −7
5) 18
6) 2
7) 10
8) −14
9) 1
10) 33
11) 1
12) −8
13) −5
14) 0
15) −176

6–6 Evaluating Two Variables

1) 21
2) 39
3) 64
4) 26
5) 45
6) −111
7) 56
8) 6
9) 58
10) 17

6–7 Combining like Terms

1) 2x − 3
2) −4x + 12
3) 9x + 3
4) −15x − 28
5) 2x − 5
6) −11x
7) 23x + 42
8) −21x
9) −2x − 12
10) 4x + 8
11) −14x
12) −x + 8
13) 10x − 6
14) 42x − 5
15) 24x + 6
16) −27x
17) 9x − 9
18) x
19) 2x + 12
20) 12x − 9
21) x

6–8 Simplifying Polynomial Expressions

1) $-14x^6 + 19x^5$
2) $2x^5 + 8x^4 + x + 12$
3) $-33x^4 + 29x^3 + 10x^2$
4) $-7x^3 - x^2 + 34$
5) $4x^5 - 5x^3 + 8x^2$
6) $5x^3 + x^2 - 12x + 1$
7) $-14x^3 + 10x^2$
8) $6x^4 - 6x$
9) $x^2 - 3$
10) $-5x - 4$
11) $2x^4 + 18x^3$
12) $9x^3 + 18$
13) $-3x^3 + 7x^2 - 3$
14) $32x^3 - 14x^2$
15) $-6x^3$

Chapter 7: Equations

7-1 One– Step Equations

7-2 One– Step Equation Word Problems

7-3 Two– Step Equations

7-4 Two– Step Equation Word Problems

7-5 Multi– Step Equations

7–1 One–Step Equations

Solve each equation.

1) $x + 3 = 17$

2) $22 = (-8) + x$

3) $3x = (-30)$

4) $(-36) = (-6x)$

5) $(-6) = 4 + x$

6) $2 + x = (-2)$

7) $20x = (-220)$

8) $18 = x + 5$

9) $(-23) + x = (-19)$

10) $5x = (-45)$

11) $x - 12 = (-25)$

12) $x - 3 = (-12)$

13) $(-35) = x - 27$

14) $8 = 2x$

15) $(-6x) = 36$

16) $(-55) = (-5x)$

17) $x - 30 = 20$

18) $8x = 32$

19) $36 = (-4x)$

20) $4x = 68$

21) $30x = 300$

7–2 One–Step Equation Word Problems

Solve.

1) How many boxes of envelopes can you buy with $18 if one box costs $3?

2) After paying $6.25 for a salad, Ella has $45.56. How much money did she have before buying the salad?

3) How many packages of diapers can you buy with $50 if one package costs $5?

4) Last week James ran 20 miles more than Michael. James ran 56 miles. How many miles did Michael run?

5) Last Friday Jacob had $32.52. Over the weekend he received some money for cleaning the attic. He now has $44. How much money did he receive?

6) After paying $10.12 for a sandwich, Amelia has $35.50. How much money did she have before buying the sandwich?

7–3 Two–Step Equations

Solve each equation.

1) $5(8 + x) = 20$

2) $(-7)(x - 9) = 42$

3) $(-12)(2x - 3) = (-12)$

4) $6(1 + x) = 12$

5) $12(2x + 4) = 60$

6) $7(3x + 2) = 42$

7) $8(14 + 2x) = (-34)$

8) $(-15)(2x - 4) = 48$

9) $3(x + 5) = 12$

10) $\dfrac{3x - 12}{6} = 4$

11) $(-12) = \dfrac{x + 15}{6}$

12) $110 = (-5)(2x - 6)$

13) $\dfrac{x}{8} - 12 = 4$

14) $20 = 12 + \dfrac{x}{4}$

15) $\dfrac{-24 + x}{6} = (-12)$

16) $(-4)(5 + 2x) = (-100)$

17) $(-12x) + 20 = 32$

18) $\dfrac{-2 + 6x}{4} = (-8)$

19) $\dfrac{x + 6}{5} = (-5)$

20) $(-9) + \dfrac{x}{4} = (-15)$

7–4 Two–Step Equation Word Problems

Solve.

1) The sum of three consecutive even numbers is 48. What is the smallest of these numbers?

2) How old am I if 400 reduced by 2 times my age is 244?

3) For a field trip, 4 students rode in cars and the rest filled nine buses. How many students were in each bus if 472 students were on the trip?

4) The sum of three consecutive numbers is 72. What is the smallest of these numbers?

5) 331 students went on a field trip. Six buses were filled, and 7 students traveled in cars. How many students were in each bus?

6) You bought a magazine for $5 and four erasers. You spent a total of $25. How much did each eraser cost?

7–5 Multi–Step Equations

Solve each equation.

1) $-(2 - 2x) = 10$

2) $-12 = -(2x + 8)$

3) $3x + 15 = (-2x) + 5$

4) $-28 = (-2x) - 12x$

5) $2(1 + 2x) + 2x = -118$

6) $3x - 18 = 22 + x - 3 + x$

7) $12 - 2x = (-32) - x + x$

8) $7 - 3x - 3x = 3 - 3x$

9) $6 + 10x + 3x = (-30) + 4x$

10) $(-3x) - 8(-1 + 5x) = 352$

11) $24 = (-4x) - 8 + 8$

12) $9 = 2x - 7 + 6x$

13) $6(1 + 6x) = 294$

14) $-10 = (-4x) - 6x$

15) $4x - 2 = (-7) + 5x$

16) $5x - 14 = 8x + 4$

17) $40 = -(4x - 8)$

18) $(-18) - 6x = 6(1 + 3x)$

19) $x - 5 = -2(6 + 3x)$

20) $6 = 1 - 2x + 5$

Answers of Worksheets – Chapter 7

7–1 One–Step Equations

1) 14
2) 30
3) −10
4) 6
5) −10
6) −4
7) −11
8) 13
9) 4
10) −9
11) −13
12) −9
13) −8
14) 4
15) −6
16) 11
17) 50
18) 4
19) −9
20) 17
21) 10

7–2 One–Step Equation Word Problems

1) 6
2) $51.81
3) 10
4) 36
5) 11.48
6) 45.62

7–3 Two–Step Equations

1) −4
2) 3
3) 2
4) 1
5) 0.5
6) $\frac{4}{3}$
7) $-\frac{73}{8}$
8) $\frac{2}{5}$
9) −1
10) 12
11) −87
12) −8
13) 128
14) 32
15) −48
16) 10
17) −1
18) −5
19) −31
20) −24

7–4 Two–Step Equation Word Problems

1) 14
2) 78
3) 52
4) 23
5) 54
6) $5

7–5 Multi–Step Equations

1) 6
2) 2
3) -2
4) 2
5) -20
6) 37
7) 22
8) $\frac{4}{3}$
9) -4
10) -8
11) -6
12) 2
13) 8
14) 1
15) 5
16) -6
17) -8
18) -1
19) -1
20) 0

Chapter 8: Systems of Equations

8-1 Solving Systems of Equations by Graphing

8-2 Solving Systems of Equations by Substitution

8-3 Solving Systems of Equations by Elimination

8-4 Systems of Equations Word Problems

8-1 Solving Systems of Equations by Graphing

Solve each system of equations by graphing.

1) $y = -4x - 2$
   $y = -2x + 1$

2) $y = -8x - 4$
   $y = 2$

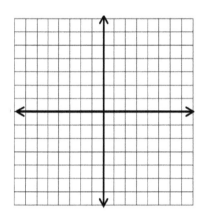
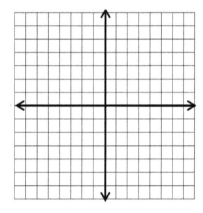

4) $y = 9x - 5$
   $y = -6x + 4$

5) $y = \frac{1}{2}x + 8$
   $y = 8x - 2$

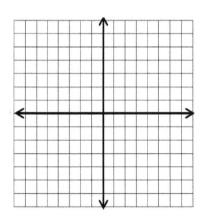
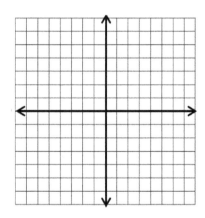

8-2 Solving Systems of Equations by Substitution

Solve each system of equation by substitution.

1) $-x - y = -13$

   $-2x + 2y = 10$

2) $-2x + 2y = 4$

   $-2x + y = 3$

3) $-10x + 2y = -6$

   $6x - 16y = 48$

4) $y = -8$

   $x - 12y = 72$

5) $2y = -6x + 10$

   $10x - 8y = -6$

6) $3x - 9y = -3$

   $3y = 3x - 3$

7) $-4x + 12y = 12$

   $-14x + 16y = -10$

8) $-10x - 16y = 34$

   $4x - 14y = -34$

8-3 Solving Systems of Equations by Elimination

Solve each system of equation by elimination.

1) $x - y = -12$
$-5x + 3y = 6$

2) $-3x - 4y = 5$
$x - 2y = 5$

3) $5x - 14y = 22$
$-6x + 7y = 3$

4) $10x - 14y = -4$
$-10x - 20y = -30$

5) $32x + 14y = 52$
$16x - 4y = -40$

6) $2x - 8y = -6$
$8x + 2y = 10$

7) $-4x + 4y = -4$
$4x + 2y = 10$

8) $4x + 6y = 10$
$8x + 12y = -20$

9) $20x - 18y = -12$
$18x - 8y = 22$

10) $8x + 10y = 52$
$8x + 6y = 44$

8-4 Systems of Equations Word Problems

1) A farmhouse shelters 10 animals, some are pigs and some are ducks. Altogether there are 36 legs. How many of each animal are there?

2) A class of 195 students went on a field trip. They took vehicles, some cars and some buses. Find the number of cars and the number of buses they took if each car holds 5 students and each bus hold 45 students.

3) The difference of two numbers is 6. Their sum is 14. Find the numbers.

4) The sum of the digits of a certain two–digit number is 7. Reversing its increasing the number by 9. What is the number?

5) The difference of two numbers is 18. Their sum is 66. Find the numbers.

Answers of Worksheets – Chapter 8

8–1 Solving Systems of Equations by Graphing

1)
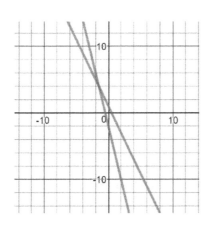

2)
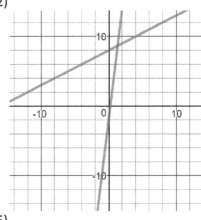

4)
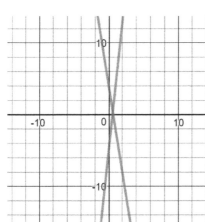

5)
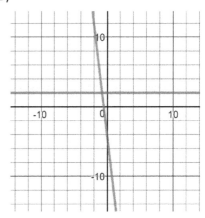

8–2 Solving Systems of Equations by Substitution

1) (4, 9)
2) (–1, 1)
3) (0, –3)
4) (–24, –8)
5) (1, 2)
6) (2, 1)
7) (3, 2)
8) (–5, 1)

8–3 Solving Systems of Equations by Elimination

1) (15, 27)
2) (1, −2)
3) (−4, −3)
4) (1, 1)
5) (−1, 6)
6) (1, 1)
7) (2, 1)
8) No solution
9) (3, 4)
10) (4, 2)

8–4 Systems of Equations Word Problems

1) There are 8 pigs and 2 ducks.
2) There are 3 cars and 4 buses.
3) 10 and 4
4) 34
5) 24 and 42

Chapter 9: Inequalities

9-1 Graphing Single– Variable Inequalities

9-2 One– Step Inequalities

9-3 Two– Step Inequalities

9-4 Multi– Step Inequalities

9-1 Graphing Single-Variable Inequalities

Draw a graph for each inequality.

1) $-2 > x$

2) $5 \leq -x$

3) $x > 7$

4) $-x > 1.5$

9-2 One-Step Inequalities

Solve each inequality and graph it.

1) $x + 9 \geq 11$

2) $x - 4 \leq 2$

3) $6x \geq 36$

4) $7 + x < 16$

5) $x + 8 \leq 1$

6) $3x > 12$

7) $3x < 24$

9-3 Two-Step Inequalities

Solve each inequality and graph it.

1) $3x - 4 \leq 5$

2) $4x - 19 < 19$

3) $3x + 6 \geq 12$

4) $6x - 5 \geq 19$

5) $2x - 3 < 21$

6) $3 + 4x < 19$

9-4 Multi-Step Inequalities

Solve each inequality and graph it.

1) $\dfrac{7x+1}{3} \geq 5$

2) $\dfrac{9x}{7} - x < 2$

3) $\dfrac{4x+8}{2} \leq 12$

4) $\dfrac{3x-8}{7} > 1$

5) $-3(x-7) > 21$

6) $4 + \dfrac{x}{3} < 7$

Answers of Worksheets – Chapter 8

9–1 Graphing Single–Variable Inequalities

1) $-2 > x$

2) $x \leq -5$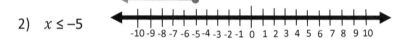

3) $x > 7$

4) $-1.5 > x$

9–2 One–Step Inequalities

1) $x + 9 \geq 11$

2) $x - 4 \leq 2$

3) $6x \geq 36$

4) $7 + x < 16$

5) $x + 8 \leq 1$

6) $3x > 12$

7) $3x < 24$

9–3 Two–Step Inequalities

1) $3x - 4 \leq 5$

2) $4x + 19 < 19$

3) $3x + 6 \geq 12$

4) $6x - 5 \geq 19$

5) $2x - 3 < 11$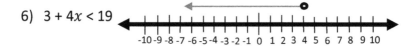

6) $3 + 4x < 19$

9–4 Multi–Step Inequalities

1) $\dfrac{7x+1}{3} \geq 5$

2) $\dfrac{9x}{7} - x < 2$

3) $\dfrac{4x+8}{2} \leq 12$

4) $\dfrac{3x-8}{7} > 1$

5) $-3(x-7) > 21$

6) $4 + \dfrac{x}{3} < 7$

Chapter 10: Linear Functions

10-1 Finding Slope

10-2 Graphing Lines Using Slope– Intercept Form

10-3 Graphing Lines Using Standard Form

10-4 Writing Linear Equations

10-5 Graphing Linear Inequalities

10-6 Finding Midpoint

10-7 Finding Distance of Two Points

10-1 Finding Slope

Find the slope of the line through each pair of points.

1) (2, − 10), (3, 6)

2) (4, − 6), (− 3, − 8)

3) (7, − 12), (5, 10)

4) (19, 3), (20, 3)

5) (15, 8), (− 17, 9)

6) (6, − 12), (15, − 3)

7) (3, 1), (7, − 5)

8) (3, − 2), (− 7, 8)

9) (15, − 3), (− 9, 5)

10) (− 4, 7), (− 6, − 4)

11) (6, − 8), (− 11, − 7)

12) (− 6, 13), (17, − 9)

13) (− 10, − 2), (− 6, − 5)

14) (4, 5), (− 4, 10)

15) (− 3, 1), (− 17, 2)

16) (7, 0), (− 13, − 11)

17) (17, − 13), (17, 8)

18) (12, 2), (− 7, 5)

10-2 Graphing Lines Using Slope-Intercept Form

Sketch the graph of each line.

1) $y = \dfrac{1}{2}x - 4$

2) $y = -\dfrac{3}{5}x - 7$

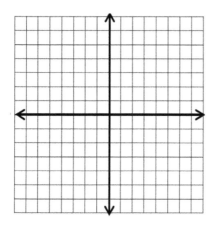
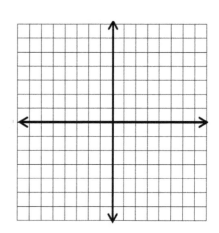

3) $y = \dfrac{1}{3}x - 8$

5) $y = 6x$

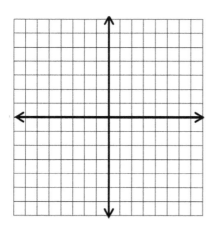
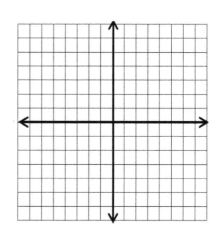

10-3 Graphing Lines Using Standard Form

Sketch the graph of each line.

1) $x + 4y = 12$

2) $2y = -2$

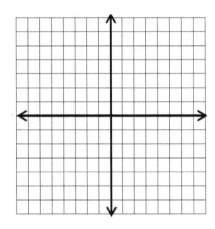
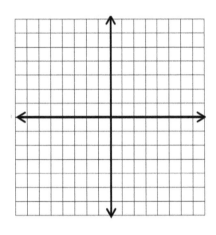

3) $2x - y = 4$

4) $x + y = 2$

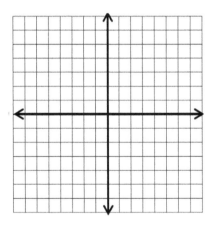
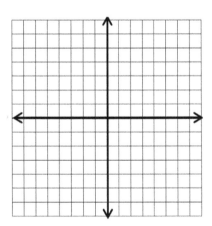

10-4 Writing Linear Equations

Write the slope–intercept form of the equation of the line through the given points.

1) through: $(-4, -2), (-3, 5)$

2) through: $(5, 4), (-4, 3)$

3) through: $(0, -2), (-5, 3)$

4) through: $(-4, -2), (-3, 5)$

5) through: $(0, 3), (-4, -1)$

6) through: $(0, 2), (1, -3)$

7) through: $(0, -5), (4, 3)$

8) through: $(-1, 4), (0, 4)$

9) through: $(2, -3), (3, -5)$

10) through: $(2, 5), (-1, -4)$

11) through: $(1, -3), (-3, 1)$

12) through: $(3, 3), (1, -5)$

13) through: $(4, 4), (3, -5)$

14) through: $(0, 3), (1, 1)$

15) through: $(5, 5), (2, -3)$

16) through: $(-2, -2), (2, -5)$

17) through: $(-3, -2), (1, -1)$

18) through: $(1, 5), (4, 1)$

10-5 Graphing Linear Inequalities

Sketch the graph of each linear inequality.

1) $y < -4x + 2$

2) $2x + y < -4$

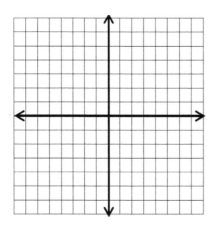
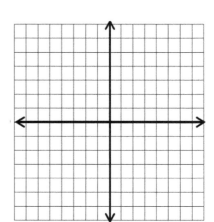

3) $x - 3y < -5$

4) $6x - 2y \geq 8$

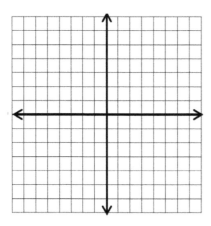
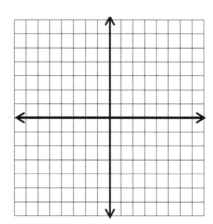

10-6 Finding Midpoint

Find the midpoint of the line segment with the given endpoints.

1) (3, 9), (− 1, 6)

2) (2, − 2), (3, − 5)

3) (− 2, 6), (− 3, − 2)

4) (0, 2), (− 2, − 6)

5) (7, 4), (9, − 1)

6) (4, − 5), (0, 8)

7) (1, − 2), (1, − 6)

8) (− 2, − 3), (3, − 6)

9) (7, 0), (− 7, 5)

10) (− 2, 6), (− 3, − 2)

11) (− 1, 1), (5, − 5)

12) (2.3, − 1.3), (− 2.2, − 0.5)

13) (4.1, 6.32), (4, 5.6)

14) (2, − 1), (− 6, 0)

15) (− 4, 4), (5, − 1)

16) (− 2, − 3), (− 6, 5)

17) ($\frac{1}{2}$, 1), (2, 4)

18) (− 2.9, − 2.958), (8.6, 5)

10-7 Finding Distance of Two Points

Find the distance between each pair of points.

1) (− 1, 2), (− 1, − 7)

2) (6, −2), (1, 10)

3) (− 8, − 5), (− 5, −1)

4) (− 6, − 10), (− 2, − 10)

5) (4, − 6), (− 5, 6)

6) (− 6, − 7), (0, 1)

7) (− 4, 5), (8, − 10)

8) (8, 4), (3, − 8)

9) (10, −8), (0, 16)

10) (4, 6), (− 4, − 9)

11) (− 3, − 5), (6, 7)

12) (− 7, − 2), (− 2, 10)

13) (5, 3), (1, 0)

14) (− 3, 7), (9, −8)

15) (− 6, 12), (−3, 8)

16) (− 21, 5), (− 3, 5)

17) (0, 8), (4, 11)

18) (6, 4), (− 6, − 1)

Answers of Worksheets – Chapter 9

10–1 Finding Slope

1) 16
2) $\frac{2}{7}$
3) −11
4) 0
5) $-\frac{1}{32}$
6) 1
7) $-\frac{3}{2}$
8) −1
9) $-\frac{1}{3}$
10) $\frac{11}{2}$
11) $-\frac{1}{17}$
12) $-\frac{22}{23}$
13) $-\frac{3}{4}$
14) $-\frac{5}{8}$
15) $-\frac{1}{14}$
16) $\frac{11}{20}$
17) Undefined
18) $-\frac{3}{19}$

10–2 Graphing Lines Using Slope–Intercept Form

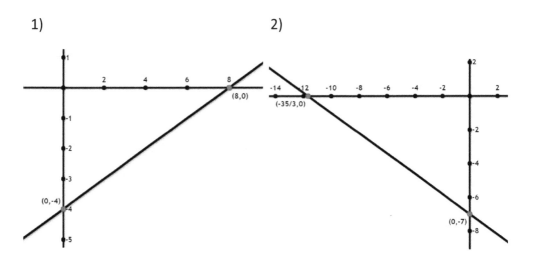

3)   4)

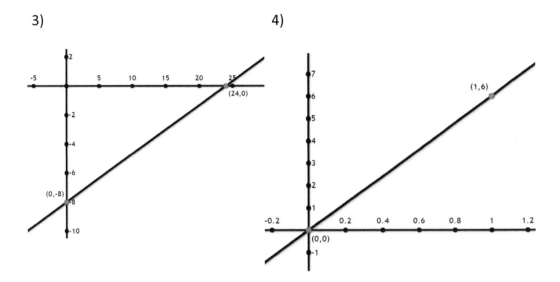

10–3 Graphing Lines Using Standard Form

1)

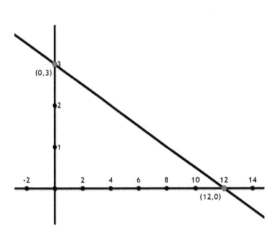

2)

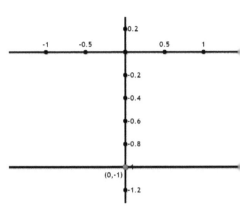

3)

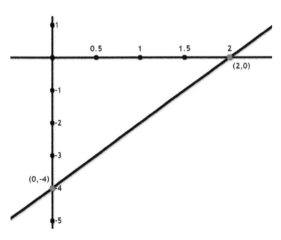

4)

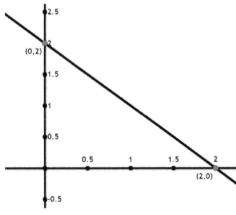

10–4 Writing Linear Equations

1) $y = 7x + 26$
2) $y = \frac{1}{9}x + \frac{31}{9}$
3) $y = -x - 2$
4) $y = -x + 2$
5) $y = x + 3$
6) $y = -5x + 2$
7) $y = 2x - 5$
8) $y = 4$
9) $y = -2x + 1$
10) $y = 3x - 1$
11) $y = -x - 2$
12) $y = 4x - 9$
13) $y = 9x - 32$
14) $y = -2x + 3$
15) $y = \frac{8}{3}x - \frac{25}{3}$
16) $y = -\frac{3}{4}x - \frac{7}{2}$
17) $y = \frac{1}{4}x - \frac{5}{4}$
18) $y = -\frac{4}{3}x + \frac{19}{3}$

10–5 Graphing Linear Inequalities

1)
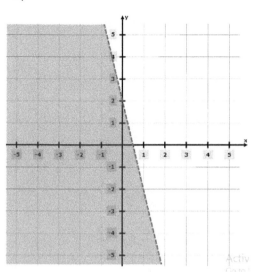

2)
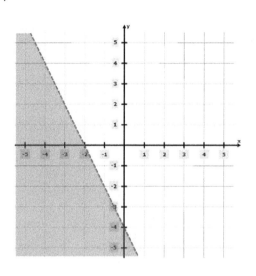

3)
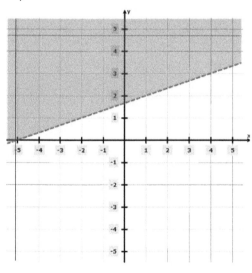

4)
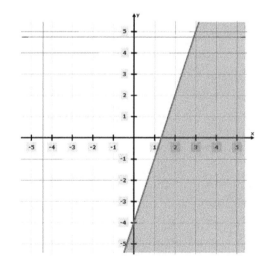

10–6 Finding Midpoint

1) (1, 7.5)
2) (2.5, −3.5)
3) (−2.5, 2)
4) (−1, −2)
5) (8, 1.5)
6) (2, 1.5)
7) (1, − 4)
8) (0.5, − 4.5)
9) (0, 2.5)
10) (−2.5, 2)
11) (2, −2)
12) (0.05, −0.9)
13) (4.05, 5.96)
14) (−2, − 0.5)
15) (0.5, 1.5)
16) (−4, 1)
17) (1.25, 2.5)
18) (2.85, 1.021)

10–7 Finding Distance of Two Points

1) 9
2) 13
3) 5
4) 4
5) 15
6) 10
7) 20
8) 13
9) 26
10) 17
11) 15
12) 13
13) 5
14) 20
15) 5
16) 18
17) 5
18) 13

Chapter 11: Polynomials

11-1 Writing Polynomials in Standard Form

11-2 Simplifying Polynomials

11-3 Adding and Subtracting Polynomials

11-4 Multiplying Monomials

11-5 Multiplying and Dividing Monomials

11-6 Multiplying a Polynomial and a Monomial

11-7 Multiplying Binomials

11-8 Factoring Trinomials

11-9 Operations with Polynomials

11-1 Writing Polynomials in Standard Form

Write each polynomial in standard form.

1) $3x^2 - 5x^3$

2) $3 + 4x^3 - 3$

3) $2x^2 + 1x - 6x^3$

4) $9x - 7x$

5) $12 - 7x + 9x^4$

6) $5x^2 + 13x - 2x^3$

7) $-3 + 16x - 16x$

8) $3x(x + 4) - 2(x + 4)$

9) $(x + 5)(x - 2)$

10) $3x^2 + x + 12 - 5x^2 - 2x$

11) $12x^5 + 7x^3 - 3x^5 - 8x^3$

12) $3x(2x + 5 - 2x^2)$

13) $11x(x^5 + 2x^3)$

14) $(x + 6)(x + 3)$

15) $(x + 4)^2$

16) $(8x - 7)(3x + 2)$

17) $5x(3x^2 + 2x + 1)$

18) $7x(3 - x + 6x^3)$

11-2 Simplifying Polynomials

Simplify each expression.

1) $11 - 4x^2 + 3x^2 - 7x^3 + 3$

2) $2x^5 - x^3 + 8x^2 - 2x^5$

3) $(-5)(x^6 + 10) - 8(14 - x^6)$

4) $4(2x^2 + 4x^2 - 3x^3) + 6x^3 + 17$

5) $11 - 6x^2 + 5x^2 - 12x^3 + 22$

6) $2x^2 - 2x + 3x^3 + 12x - 22x$

7) $(3x - 8)(3x - 4)$

8) $(12x + 2y)^2$

9) $(12x^3 + 28x^2 + 10x + 4) \div (x + 2)$

10) $(2x + 12x^2 - 2) \div (x + 2)$

11) $(2x^3 - 1) + (3x^3 - 2x^3)$

12) $(x - 5)(x - 3)$

13) $(3x + 8)(3x - 8)$

14) $(8x^2 - 3x) - (5x - 5 - 8x^2)$

11-3 Adding and Subtracting Polynomials

Simplify each expression.

1) $(2x^3 - 2) + (2x^3 + 2)$

2) $(4x^3 + 5) - (7 - 2x^3)$

3) $(4x^2 + 2x^3) - (2x^3 + 5)$

4) $(4x^2 - x) + (3x - 5x^2)$

5) $(7x + 9) - (3x + 9)$

6) $(4x^4 - 2x) - (6x - 2x^4)$

7) $(12x - 4x^3) - (8x^3 + 6x)$

8) $(2x^3 - 8x^2) - (5x^2 - 3x^3)$

9) $(2x^2 - 6) + (9x^2 - 4x^3)$

10) $(4x^3 + 3x^4) - (x^4 - 5x^3)$

11) $(-12x^4 + 10x^5 + 2x^3) + (14x^3 + 23x^5 + 8x^4)$

12) $(13x^2 - 6x^5 - 2x) - (-10x^2 - 11x^5 + 9x)$

13) $(35 + 9x^5 - 3x^2) + (8x^4 + 3x^5) - (27 - 5x^4)$

14) $(3x^5 - 2x^3 - 4x) + (4x + 10x^4 - 23) + (x^2 - x^3 + 12)$

11-4 Multiplying Monomials

Simplify each expression.

1) $2xy^2z \times 4z^2$

2) $4xy \times x^2y$

3) $4pq^3 \times (-2p^4q)$

4) $8s^4t^2 \times st^5$

5) $12p^3 \times (-3p^4)$

6) $-4p^2q^3r \times 6pq^2r^3$

7) $(-8a^4) \times (-12a^6b)$

8) $3u^4v^2 \times (-7u^2v^3)$

9) $4u^3 \times (-2u)$

10) $-6xy^2 \times 3x^2y$

11) $12y^2z^3 \times (-y^2z)$

12) $5a^2bc^2 \times 2abc^2$

11-5 Multiplying and Dividing Monomials

Simplify.

1) $(-3x^2)(8x^4y^{12})$

2) $(7x^4y^6)(4x^3y^4)$

3) $(15x^4)(3x^9)$

4) $(12x^2y^9)(7x^9y^{12})$

5) $\dfrac{36\,x^5y^7}{4\,x^4y^5}$

6) $\dfrac{80\,x^{12}y^9}{10\,x^6y^7}$

7) $\dfrac{95\,x^{18}y^7}{5\,x^9y^2}$

8) $\dfrac{200\,x^3y^8}{40\,x^3y^7}$

9) $\dfrac{-15\,x^{17}y^{13}}{3\,x^6y^9}$

10) $\dfrac{-64\,x^8y^{10}}{8\,x^3y^7}$

11-6 Multiplying a Polynomial and a Monomial

Find each product.

1) $5(3x - 6y)$

2) $9x(2x + 4y)$

3) $8x(7x - 4)$

4) $12x(3x + 9)$

5) $11x(2x - 11y)$

6) $2x(6x - 6y)$

7) $3x(2x^2 - 3x + 8)$

8) $13x(4x + 8y)$

9) $20(2x^2 - 8x - 5)$

10) $3x(3x - 2)$

11) $6x^3(3x^2 - 2x + 2)$

12) $8x^2(3x^2 - 5xy + 7y^2)$

13) $2x^2(3x^2 - 5x + 12)$

14) $2x^3(2x^2 + 5x - 4)$

15) $5x(6x^2 - 5xy + 2y^2)$

16) $9(x^2 + xy - 8y^2)$

11-7 Multiplying Binomials

Simplify each expression.

1) $(3x - 2)(4x + 2)$

2) $(2x - 5)(x + 7)$

3) $(x + 2)(x + 8)$

4) $(x^2 + 2)(x^2 - 2)$

5) $(x - 2)(x + 4)$

6) $(x - 8)(2x + 8)$

7) $(5x - 4)(3x + 3)$

8) $(x - 7)(x - 6)$

9) $(6x + 9)(4x + 9)$

10) $(2x - 6)(5x + 6)$

11) $(x - 7)(x + 7)$

12) $(x + 4)(4x - 8)$

13) $(6x - 4)(6x + 4)$

14) $(x - 7)(x + 2)$

15) $(x - 8)(x + 8)$

16) $(3x + 3)(3x - 4)$

17) $(x + 3)(x + 3)$

18) $(x + 4)(x + 6)$

11-8 Factoring Trinomials

Factor each trinomial.

1) $x^2 - 7x + 12$

2) $x^2 + 5x - 14$

3) $x^2 - 11x - 42$

4) $6x^2 + x - 12$

5) $x^2 - 17x + 30$

6) $x^2 + 8x + 15$

7) $3x^2 + 11x - 4$

8) $x^2 - 6x - 27$

9) $10x^2 + 33x - 7$

10) $x^2 + 24x + 144$

11) $49x^2 + 28xy + 4y^2$

12) $16x^2 - 40x + 25$

13) $x^2 - 10x + 25$

14) $25x^2 - 20x + 4$

15) $x^3 + 6x^2y^2 + 9xy^3$

16) $9x^2 + 24x + 16$

17) $x^2 - 8x + 16$

18) $x^2 + 121 + 22x$

11-9 Operations with Polynomials

Find each product.

1) $3x^2 (6x - 5)$

2) $5x^2 (7x - 2)$

3) $-3 (8x - 3)$

4) $6x^3 (-3x + 4)$

5) $9 (6x + 2)$

6) $8 (3x + 7)$

7) $5 (6x - 1)$

8) $-7x^4 (2x - 4)$

9) $8 (x^2 + 2x - 3)$

10) $4 (4x^2 - 2x + 1)$

11) $2 (3x^2 + 2x - 2)$

12) $8x (5x^2 + 3x + 8)$

13) $(9x + 1)(3x - 1)$

14) $(4x + 5)(6x - 5)$

15) $(7x + 3)(5x - 6)$

16) $(3x - 4)(3x + 8)$

Name each polynomial by degree and number of terms.

17) 7

18) $2x^2 - 9x - 5$

19) $-3x$

20) $-7 + 7x^3 - x^2$

21) $-8x^4 - 8x^2$

22) $3x^6 + 3x^5 - 5x^4 - 3x^2 + 2$

Answers of Worksheets – Chapter 10

10–1 Writing Polynomials in Standard Form

1) $-5x^3 + 3x^2$
2) $4x^3$
3) $-6x^3 + 2x^2 + x$
4) $2x$
5) $9x^4 - 7x + 12$
6) $-2x^3 + 5x^2 + 13x$
7) -3
8) $3x^2 + 10x - 8$
9) $x^2 + 3x - 10$
10) $-2x^2 - x + 12$
11) $9x^5 - x^3$
12) $-6x^3 + 6x^2 + 15x$
13) $11x^6 + 22x^4$
14) $x^2 + 9x + 18$
15) $x^2 + 8x + 16$
16) $24x^2 - 5x - 14$
17) $15x^3 + 10x^2 + 5x$
18) $7x^4 - 7x^2 + 21x$

10–2 Simplifying Polynomials

1) $-7x^3 - x^2 + 14$
2) $-3x^3 + 8x^2$
3) $3x^6 - 162$
4) $-6x^3 + 24x^2 + 17$
5) $-12x^3 - x^2 + 33$
6) $3x^3 + 2x^2 - 12x$
7) $9x^2 - 36x + 32$
8) $144x^2 + 48xy + 4y^2$
9) $12x^2 + 4x + 2$
10) $12x - 22 + \frac{42}{x+2}$
11) $3x^3 - 1$
12) $x^2 - 8x + 15$
13) $9x^2 - 64$
14) $16x^2 - 8x + 5$

10–3 Adding and Subtracting Polynomials

1) $4x^3$
2) $6x^3 - 2$
3) $4x^2 - 5$
4) $-x^2 + 2x$

5) $4x$

6) $6x^4 - 8x$

7) $-12x^3 + 6x$

8) $5x^3 - 13x^2$

9) $-4x^3 + 11x^2 - 6$

10) $2x^4 + 9x^3$

11) $33x^5 - 4x^4 + 16x^3$

12) $5x^5 + 23x^2 - 11x$

13) $12x^5 + 13x^4 - 3x^2 + 8$

14) $3x^5 + 10x^4 - 3x^3 + x^2 - 11$

10–4 Multiplying Monomials

1) $8xy^2z^3$

2) $4x^3y^2$

3) $-8p^5q^4$

4) $8s^5t^7$

5) $-36p^7$

6) $-24p^3q^5r^4$

7) $96a^{10}b$

8) $-21u^6v^5$

9) $-8u^4$

10) $-18x^3y^3$

11) $-12y^4z^4$

12) $10a^3b^2c^4$

10–5 Multiplying and Dividing Monomials

1) $-24x^6y^{12}$

2) $28x^7y^{10}$

3) $45x^{13}$

4) $84x^{11}y^{21}$

5) $9xy^2$

6) $8x^6y^2$

7) $19x^9y^5$

8) $5y$

9) $-5x^{11}y^4$

10) $-8x^5y^3$

10–6 Multiplying a Polynomial and a Monomial

1) $15x - 30y$

2) $18x^2 + 36xy$

3) $56x^2 - 32x$

4) $36x^2 + 108x$

5) $22x^2 - 121xy$

6) $12x^2 - 12xy$

7) $6x^3 - 9x^2 + 24x$

8) $52x^2 + 104xy$

9) $40x^2 - 160x - 100$

10) $9x^2 - 6x$

11) $18x^5 - 12x^4 + 12x^3$

12) $24x^4 - 40x^3y + 56y^2x^2$

13) $6x^4 - 10x^3 + 24x^2$

14) $4x^5 + 10x^4 - 8x^3$

15) $30x^3 - 25x^2y + 10xy^2$

16) $9x^2 + 9xy - 72y^2$

10–7 Multiplying Binomials

1) $12x^2 - 2x - 4$
2) $2x^2 + 9x - 35$
3) $x^2 + 10x + 16$
4) $x^4 - 4$
5) $x^2 + 2x - 8$
6) $2x^2 - 8x - 64$
7) $15x^2 + 3x - 12$
8) $x^2 - 13x + 42$
9) $24x^2 + 90x + 81$
10) $10x^2 - 18x - 36$
11) $x^2 - 49$
12) $4x^2 + 8x - 32$
13) $36x^2 - 16$
14) $x^2 - 5x - 14$
15) $x^2 - 64$
16) $9x^2 - 3x - 12$
17) $x^2 + 6x + 9$
18) $x^2 + 10x + 24$

10–8 Factoring Trinomials

1) $(x - 3)(x - 4)$
2) $(x - 2)(x + 7)$
3) $(x + 3)(x - 14)$
4) $(2x + 3)(3x - 4)$
5) $(x - 15)(x - 2)$
6) $(x + 3)(x + 5)$
7) $(3x + 1)(x - 4)$
8) $(x - 9)(x + 3)$
9) $(5x - 1)(2x + 7)$
10) $(x + 12)(x + 12)$
11) $(7x + 2y)(7x + 2y)$
12) $(4x - 5)(4x - 5)$
13) $(x - 5)(x - 5)$
14) $(5x - 2)(5x - 2)$
15) $x(x^2 + 6xy^2 + 9y^3)$
16) $(3x + 4)(3x + 4)$
17) $(x - 4)(x - 4)$
18) $(x + 11)(x + 11)$

10–9 Operations with Polynomials

1) $18x^3 - 15x^2$
2) $35x^3 - 10x^2$
3) $-24x + 9$
4) $-18x^4 + 24x^3$
5) $54x + 18$
6) $24x + 56$
7) $30x - 5$
8) $-14x^5 + 28x^4$
9) $8x^2 + 16x - 24$
10) $16x^2 - 8x + 4$
11) $6x^2 + 4x - 4$
12) $40x^3 + 24x^2 + 64x$

13) $27x^2 - 6x - 1$

14) $24x^2 + 10x - 25$

15) $35x^2 - 27x - 18$

16) $9x^2 + 12x - 32$

17) Constant monomial

18) Quadratic

19) Linear monomial

20) Cubic trinomial

21) Quartic binomial

22) Sixth degree polynomial with five terms

Chapter 12: Exponents and Radicals

12-1 Multiplication Property of Exponents

12-2 Division Property of Exponents

12-3 Powers of Products and Quotients

12-4 Zero and Negative Exponents

12-5 Negative Exponents and Negative Bases

12-6 Writing Scientific Notation

12-7 Square Roots

12-1 Multiplication Property of Exponents

Simplify.

1) $4^2 \cdot 4^2$

2) $2 \cdot 2^2 \cdot 2^2$

3) $3^2 \cdot 3^2$

4) $3x^3 \cdot x$

5) $12x^4 \cdot 3x$

6) $6x \cdot 2x^2$

7) $5x^4 \cdot 5x^4$

8) $6x^2 \cdot 6x^3y^4$

9) $7x^2y^5 \cdot 9xy^3$

10) $7xy^4 \cdot 4x^3y^3$

11) $(2x^2)^2$

12) $3x^5y^3 \cdot 8x^2y^3$

13) $7x^3 \cdot 10y^3x^5 \cdot 8yx^3$

14) $(x^4)^3$

15) $(2x^2)^4$

16) $(x^2)^3$

17) $(6x)^2$

18) $3x^4y^5 \cdot 7x^2y^3$

12-2 Division Property of Exponents

Simplify.

1) $\dfrac{5^5}{5}$

2) $\dfrac{3}{3^5}$

3) $\dfrac{2^2}{2^3}$

4) $\dfrac{2^4}{2^2}$

5) $\dfrac{x}{x^3}$

6) $\dfrac{3x^3}{9x^4}$

7) $\dfrac{2x^{-5}}{9x^{-2}}$

8) $\dfrac{21x^8}{7x^3}$

9) $\dfrac{7x^6}{4x^7}$

10) $\dfrac{6x^2}{4x^3}$

11) $\dfrac{5x}{10x^3}$

12) $\dfrac{3x^3}{2x^5}$

13) $\dfrac{12x^3}{14x^6}$

14) $\dfrac{12x^3}{9y^8}$

15) $\dfrac{25xy^4}{5x^6y^2}$

16) $\dfrac{2x^4}{7x}$

17) $\dfrac{16x^2y^8}{4x^3}$

18) $\dfrac{12x^4}{15x^7y^9}$

19) $\dfrac{12yx^4}{10yx^8}$

20) $\dfrac{16x^4y}{9x^8y^2}$

21) $\dfrac{5x^8}{20x^8}$

12-3 Powers of Products and Quotients

Simplify.

1) $(2x^3)^4$

2) $(4xy^4)^2$

3) $(5x^4)^2$

4) $(11x^5)^2$

5) $(4x^2y^4)^4$

6) $(2x^4y^4)^3$

7) $(3x^2y^2)^2$

8) $(3x^4y^3)^4$

9) $(2x^6y^8)^2$

10) $(12x\ 3x)^3$

11) $(2x^9\ x^6)^3$

12) $(5x^{10}y^3)^3$

13) $(4x^3\ x^2)^2$

14) $(3x^3\ 5x)^2$

15) $(10x^{11}y^3)^2$

16) $(9x^7\ y^5)^2$

17) $(4x^4y^6)^5$

18) $(4x^4)^2$

19) $(3x\ 4y^3)^2$

20) $(9x^2y)^3$

21) $(12x^2y^5)^2$

12-4 Zero and Negative Exponents

Evaluate the following expressions.

1) 0.8^{-2}

2) 0.2^{-4}

3) 10^{-2}

4) 0.5^{-3}

5) 22^{-1}

6) 9^{-1}

7) 3^{-2}

8) 4^{-2}

9) 5^{-2}

10) 35^{-1}

11) 6^{-3}

12) 0^{15}

13) 10^{-9}

14) 3^{-4}

15) 5^{-2}

16) 2^{-4}

17) 7^{-3}

18) 8^{-1}

19) 7^{-3}

20) 2^{-4}

21) $(\frac{2}{3})^{-2}$

22) $(\frac{1}{5})^{-3}$

23) $(\frac{5}{10})^{-8}$

24) $(\frac{2}{5})^{-3}$

12-5 Negative Exponents and Negative Bases

Simplify.

1) -6^{-1}

2) $-4x^{-3}$

3) $-\dfrac{5x}{x^{-3}}$

4) $-\dfrac{a^{-3}}{b^{-2}}$

5) $-\dfrac{5}{x^{-3}}$

6) $\dfrac{7b}{-9c^{-4}}$

7) $-\dfrac{5n^{-2}}{10p^{-3}}$

8) $\dfrac{4ab^{-2}}{-3c^{-2}}$

9) $-12x^2y^{-3}$

10) $\left(-\dfrac{1}{3}\right)^{-2}$

11) $\left(-\dfrac{3}{4}\right)^{-2}$

12) $\left(\dfrac{3a}{2c}\right)^{-2}$

13) $\left(-\dfrac{5x}{3yz}\right)^{-3}$

14) $-\dfrac{2x}{a^{-4}}$

12-6 Writing Scientific Notation

Write each number in scientific notation.

1) 91×10^3

2) 60

3) 2000000

4) 0.0000006

5) 354000

6) 0.000325

7) 2.5

8) 0.00023

9) 56000000

10) 2000000

11) 78000000

12) 0.0000022

13) 0.00012

14) 0.004

15) 78

16) 1600

17) 1450

18) 130000

19) 60

20) 0.113

21) 0.02

12-7 Square Roots

Find the value each square root.

1) $\sqrt{1}$

2) $\sqrt{4}$

3) $\sqrt{9}$

4) $\sqrt{25}$

5) $\sqrt{16}$

6) $\sqrt{49}$

7) $\sqrt{36}$

8) $\sqrt{0}$

9) $\sqrt{64}$

10) $\sqrt{81}$

11) $\sqrt{121}$

12) $\sqrt{225}$

13) $\sqrt{144}$

14) $\sqrt{100}$

15) $\sqrt{256}$

16) $\sqrt{289}$

17) $\sqrt{324}$

18) $\sqrt{400}$

19) $\sqrt{900}$

20) $\sqrt{529}$

21) $\sqrt{90}$

Answers of Worksheets – Chapter 12

12–1 Multiplication Property of Exponents

1) 4^4
2) 2^5
3) 3^4
4) $3x^4$
5) $36x^5$
6) $12x^3$
7) $25x^8$
8) $36x^5y^4$
9) $63x^3y^8$
10) $28x^4y^7$
11) $4x^4$
12) $24x^7y^6$
13) $560x^{11}y^4$
14) x^{12}
15) $16x^8$
16) x^6
17) $36x^2$
18) $21x^6y^8$

12–2 Division Property of Exponents

1) 5^4
2) $\frac{1}{3^4}$
3) $\frac{1}{2}$
4) 2^2
5) $\frac{1}{x^2}$
6) $\frac{1}{3x}$
7) $\frac{2}{9x^3}$
8) $3x^5$
9) $\frac{4}{7x}$
10) $\frac{2}{3x}$
11) $\frac{1}{2x^2}$
12) $\frac{2}{3x^2}$
13) $\frac{6}{7x^3}$
14) $\frac{3x^3}{4y^8}$
15) $\frac{5y^2}{x^5}$
16) $\frac{2x^3}{7}$
17) $\frac{4y^8}{x}$
18) $\frac{4}{5x^3y^9}$
19) $\frac{6}{5x^4}$
20) $\frac{16}{9x^4y}$
21) $\frac{1}{4}$

12–3 Powers of Products and Quotients

1) $16x^{12}$
2) $16x^2y^8$
3) $25x^8$
4) $121x^{10}$
5) $256x^8y^{16}$
6) $8x^{12}y^{12}$
7) $9x^4y^4$
8) $81x^{16}y^{12}$
9) $4x^{12}y^{16}$

10) $46.656x^6$

11) $8x^{45}$

12) $125x^{30}y^9$

13) $16x^{10}$

14) $225x^8$

15) $100x^{22}y^6$

16) $81x^{14}y^{10}$

17) $1,024x^{20}y^{30}$

18) $16x^8$

19) $144x^2y^6$

20) $729x^6y^3$

21) $144x^4y^{10}$

12–4 Zero and Negative Exponents

1) $\frac{1}{64}$

2) $\frac{1}{16}$

3) $\frac{1}{100}$

4) $\frac{1}{125}$

5) $\frac{1}{22}$

6) $\frac{1}{9}$

7) $\frac{1}{9}$

8) $\frac{1}{16}$

9) $\frac{1}{25}$

10) $\frac{1}{35}$

11) $\frac{1}{216}$

12) 0

13) $\frac{1}{1000000000}$

14) $\frac{1}{81}$

15) $\frac{1}{25}$

16) $\frac{1}{8}$

17) $\frac{1}{27}$

18) $\frac{1}{8}$

19) $\frac{1}{343}$

20) $\frac{1}{36}$

21) $\frac{9}{4}$

22) 125

23) 256

24) $\frac{125}{8}$

12–5 Negative Exponents and Negative Bases

1) $-\frac{1}{6}$

2) $-\frac{4}{x^3}$

3) $-5x^4$

4) $-\frac{b^2}{a^3}$

5) $-5x^3$

6) $-\frac{7bc^4}{9}$

7) $-\frac{p^3}{2n^2}$

8) $-\frac{4ac^2}{3b^2}$

9) $-\frac{12x^2}{y^3}$

10) 9

11) $\frac{16}{9}$

12) $\frac{4c^2}{9a^2}$

13) $-\frac{27y^3z^3}{125x^3}$

14) $-2xa^4$

12–6 Writing Scientific Notation

1) 9.1×10^4
2) 6×10^1
3) 2×10^6
4) 6×10^{-7}
5) 3.54×10^5
6) 3.25×10^{-4}
7) 2.5×10^0
8) 2.3×10^{-4}
9) 5.6×10^7
10) 2×10^6
11) 7.8×10^7
12) 2.2×10^{-6}
13) 1.2×10^{-4}
14) 4×10^{-3}
15) 7.8×10^1
16) 1.6×10^3
17) 1.45×10^3
18) 1.3×10^5
19) 6×10^1
20) 1.13×10^{-1}
21) 2×10^{-2}

12–7 Square Roots

1) 1
2) 2
3) 3
4) 5
5) 4
6) 7
7) 6
8) 0
9) 8
10) 9
11) 11
12) 15
13) 12
14) 10
15) 16
16) 17
17) 18
18) 20
19) 30
20) 23
21) $3\sqrt{10}$

Chapter 13: Geometry

13-1 The Pythagorean Theorem

13-2 Classifying Triangles and Quadrilaterals

13-3 Area of Triangles

13-4 Perimeter of Polygons

13-5 Area and Circumference of Circles

13-6 Area of Squares, Rectangles, and Parallelograms

13-7 Area of Trapezoids

13-1 The Pythagorean Theorem

Do the following lengths form a right triangle?

1)
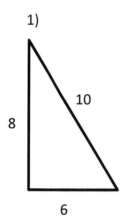

2) 3)
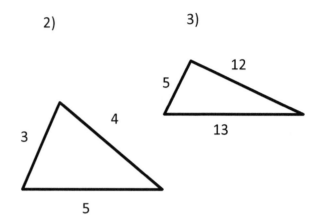

Find each missing length to the nearest tenth.

4)
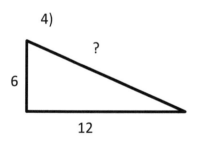

5)
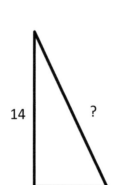

6)
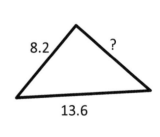

13-2 Classifying Triangles and Quadrilaterals

Classify each triangle by its angles and sides.

1) 2) 3) 4)

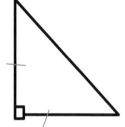

Classify each quadrilateral with the name that best describes it.

5)

7)

6)

8)

13-3 Area of Triangles

Find the area of each.

1)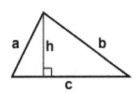

c = 9 mi

h = 3.7 mi

2)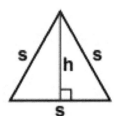

s = 14 m

h = 8 m

3)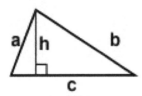

a = 5 m

b = 11 m

c = 14 m

h = 4 m

4)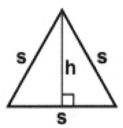

s = 16 m

h = 12.1 m

13-4 Perimeter of Polygons

Find the perimeter of each shape.

1)
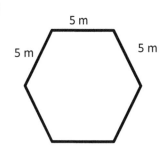

2)
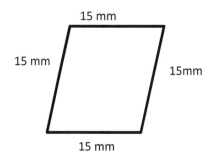

3)
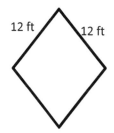

4)
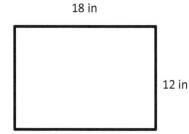

5)
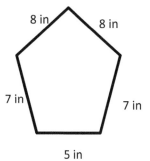

6)
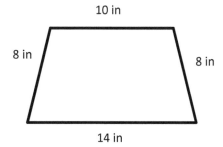

13-5 Area and Circumference of Circles

Find the area and circumference of each.

1)

2)

3)
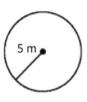

4)
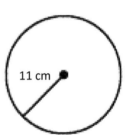

5)

6)
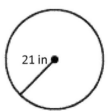

13-6 Area of Squares, Rectangles, and Parallelograms

Find the area of each.

1)
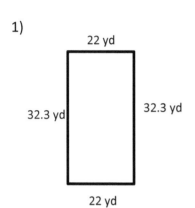

2)
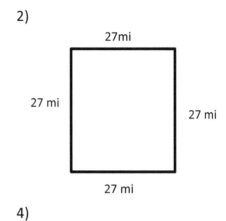

3)
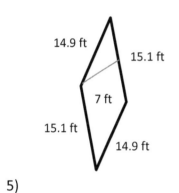

4)
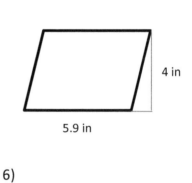

5)
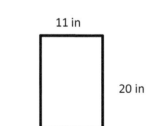

6)
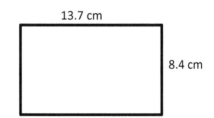

13-7 Area of Trapezoids

Calculate the area for each trapezoid.

1)
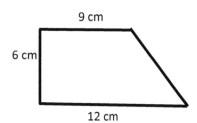

2)
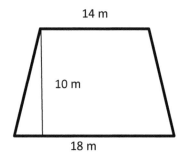

3)
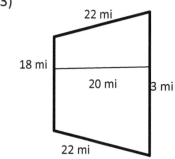

4)
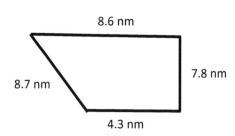

5)
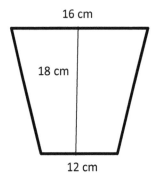

6)
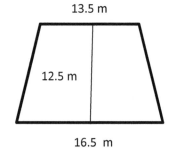

Answers of Worksheets – Chapter 13

13–1 The Pythagorean Theorem

1) yes
2) yes
3) yes
4) 17
5) 26
6) 13

13–2 Classifying Triangles and Quadrilaterals

1) Right isosceles
2) Equilateral
3) Acute isosceles
4) Obtuse scalene
5) Square
6) Trapezoid
7) Rhombus
8) Trapezoid

13–3 Area of Triangles

1) 16.65 mi^2
2) 24.49 m^2
3) 84.8 m^2
4) 45.5 yd^2
5) 136.4 km^2
6) 110.85 m^2

13–4 Perimeter of Polygons

1) 30 m
2) 60 mm
3) 48 ft
4) 60 in
5) 35 in
6) 40 in

13–5 Area and Circumference of Circles

1) Area: 50.27 in^2, Circumference: 25.12 in
2) Area: $1{,}017.36 \text{ cm}^2$, Circumference: 113.04 cm
3) Area: 78.5 m^2, Circumference: 31.4 m
4) Area: 379.94 cm^2, Circumference: 69.08 cm
5) Area: 200.96 km^2, Circumference: 50.2 km
6) Area: $1{,}384.74 \text{ km}^2$, Circumference: 131.88 km

13–6 Area of Squares, Rectangles, and Parallelograms

1) 710.6 yd^2
2) 729 mi^2
3) 105.7 ft^2
4) 23.6 in^2
5) 220 in^2
6) 115.08 cm^2

13–7 Area of Trapezoids

1) 63 cm^2
2) 192 m^2
3) 451 mi^2
4) 50.31 nm^2
5) 280 cm^2
6) 180 m^2

Chapter 14: Solid Figures

14–1 Classifying Solids

14–2 Volume of Cubes and Rectangle Prisms

14–3 Surface Area of Cubes

14–4 Surface Area of a Prism

14–5 Surface Area of a Cylinder

14–6 Surface Area of Pyramids and Cones

14–7 Surface Area of a Sphere

14–8 Volume of a Pyramid and Cone

14–9 Volume of a Sphere

14-1 Classifying Solids

Identify the names of the following shapes.

1)
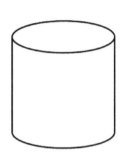

2)
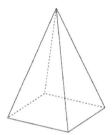

3)

4)
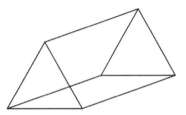

5)
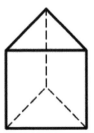

6)

14-2 Volume of Cubes and Rectangle Prisms

Find the volume of each of the rectangular prisms.

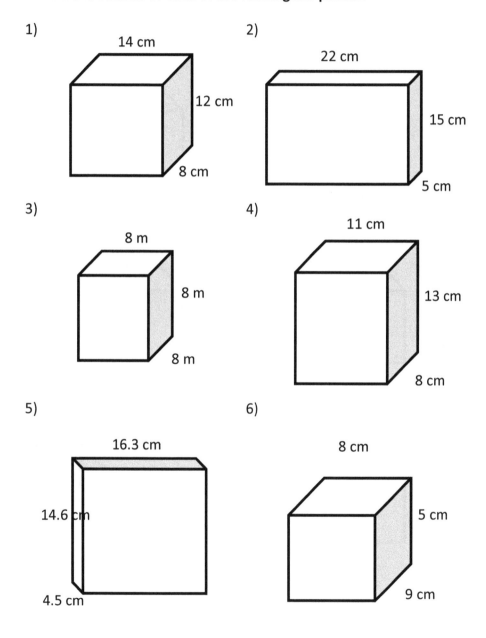

14-3 Surface Area of Cubes

Find the surface of each prism.

1)
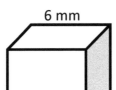

2)
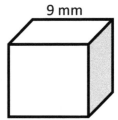

3)
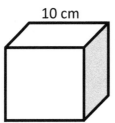

4)
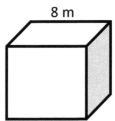

5)
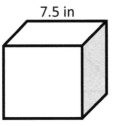

6)
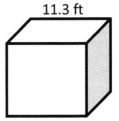

14-4 Surface Area of a Prism

Find the surface of each prism.

1)

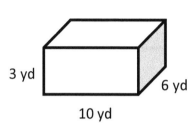

2)

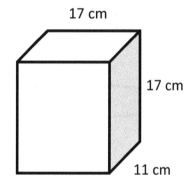

3)

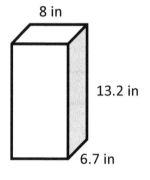

4)

(see figure)

5)

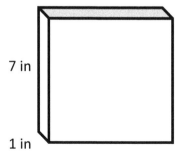

6)

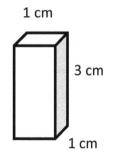

14-5 Surface Area of a Cylinder

Find the surface of each cylinder.

1)

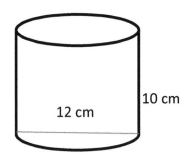

2)

3)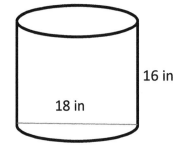

4)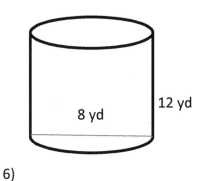

5)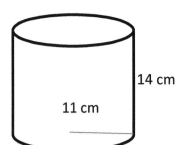

6)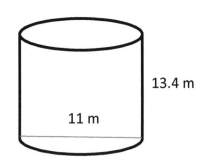

14-6 Surface Area of Pyramids and Cones

Find the surface area of each figure.

1)

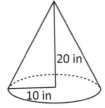

2)

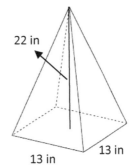

3)

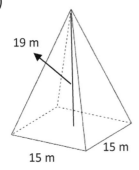

4)

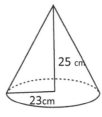

5)

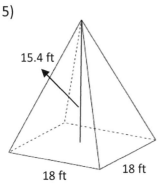

6)

14-7 Surface Area of a Sphere

Find the surface area of each figure. Round your answer to near tenth.

1)
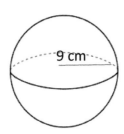

2)
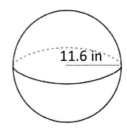

3)
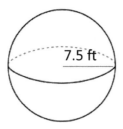

4)
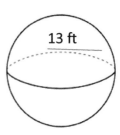

5)

6)
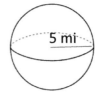

14-8 Volume of a Pyramid and Cone

Find the volume of each figure.

1)
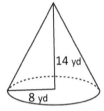

2)
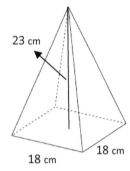

3)
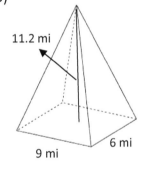

4)
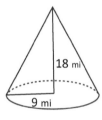

5)
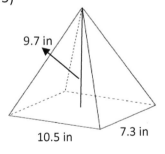

6)
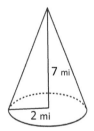

14-9 Volume of a Sphere

Find the volume of each figure.

1)

2)

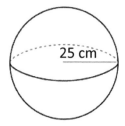

3)

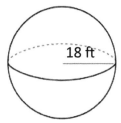

4)

5)

6)

Answers of Worksheets – Chapter 14

14–1 Classifying Solids

1) Cylinder
2) Triangular pyramid
3) Rectangular prism
4) Triangular pyramid
5) Triangular prism
6) Cylinder

14–2 Volume of Cubes and Rectangle Prisms

1) 1344 cm^3
2) 1650 cm^3
3) 512 m^3
4) 1144 cm^3
5) 1070.91 m^3
6) 360 m^3

14–3 Surface Area of a Cube

1) 216
2) 486
3) 600
4) 384
5) 337.5
6) 766.14

14–4 Surface Area of a Prism

1) 216 yd^2
2) 294 mm^2
3) 495.28 in^2
4) 1326 cm^2
5) 126 in^2
6) 14 cm^2

14–5 Surface Area of a Cylinder

1) 301.714 ft^2
2) 603.43 cm^2
3) 1414.29 in^2
4) 402.12 yd^2
5) 1728.57 cm^2
6) 653.4 m^2

14–6 Surface Area of Pyramids and Cones

1) 942.48 in^3
2) 596.444 in^2
3) 612.8 m^3
4) 468.32 m^3
5) 642.1334 ft^2
6) 233.7 km^2

14–7 Surface Area of a Sphere

1) 1018.29 cm^2
2) 1691.61 in^2
3) 707.1429 ft^2
4) 2124.57 ft^2
5) 154 mm^2
6) 314.29 mi^2

14–8 Volume of a Pyramid and Cone

1) 938.3 yd^3
2) 2484 cm^3
3) 201.6 mi^3
4) 1526.8 mi^3
5) 247.835 in^3
6) 29.3 mi^3

14–9 Volume of a Sphere

1) 137,258.28 cm^3
2) 65,449.85 cm^3
3) 24,429.024 ft^3
4) 9,202.78 cm^3
5) 3,053.63 in^3
6) 523.6 in^3

Chapter 15: Statistics

15-1 Mean, Median, Mode, and Range of the Given Data

15-2 Bar Graph

15-3 Box and Whisker Plots

15-4 Stem– And– Leaf Plot

15-5 The Pie Graph or Circle Graph

15-6 Scatter Plots

15-7 Probability

15-1 Mean, Median, Mode, and Range of the Given Data

Write Mean, Median, Mode, and Range of the Given Data.

1) 7, 2, 5, 1, 1, 2

2) 2, 2, 2, 3, 6, 3, 7, 4

3) 9, 4, 3, 1, 7, 9, 4, 6, 4

4) 8, 4, 2, 4, 3, 2, 4, 5

5) 8, 5, 7, 5, 7, 9, 8

6) 5, 1, 4, 4, 9, 2, 9, 2, 5, 1

7) 4, 1, 5, 9, 7, 7, 5, 4, 3, 5

8) 7, 5, 4, 9, 6, 7, 7, 5, 2

9) 2, 5, 5, 6, 2, 4, 7, 6, 4, 9

10) 10, 5, 2, 5, 4, 5, 8, 10

11) 5, 1, 5, 2, 2

12) 2, 3, 5, 9, 6

15-2 Bar Graph

Graph the given information as a bar graph.

Day	Hot dogs sold
Monday	90
Tuesday	70
Wednesday	30
Thursday	20
Friday	60

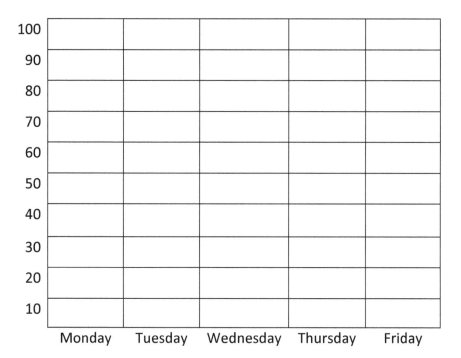

15-3 Box and Whisker Plots

Make box and whisker plots for the given data.

1) 73, 84, 86, 95, 68, 67, 100, 94, 77, 80, 62, 79

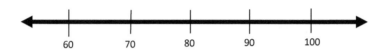

2) 11, 17, 22, 18, 23, 2, 3, 16, 21, 7, 8, 15, 5

3) 20, 12, 1, 24, 14, 23, 8, 2, 22, 12, 3

15-4 Stem-And-Leaf Plot

Make stem ad leaf plots for the given data.

1) 74, 88, 97, 72, 79, 86, 95, 79, 83, 91

   Key: 8 / 6 =

   Stem | Leaf plot

2) 37, 48, 26, 33, 49, 26, 19, 26, 48

   Key: 3 / 7 =

   Stem | Leaf plot

3) 58, 41, 42, 67, 54, 65, 65, 54, 69, 53

   Key: 6 / 5 =

   Stem | Leaf plot

15-5 The Pie Graph or Circle Graph

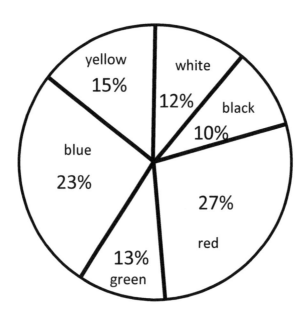

Favorite colors

1) Which color is most?

2) What percentage of pie graph is yellow?

3) Which color is least?

4) What percentage of pie graph is blue?

5) What percentage of pie graph is green?

15-6 Scatter Plots

Construct a scatter plot.

X	Y
1	20
2	40
3	50
4	60

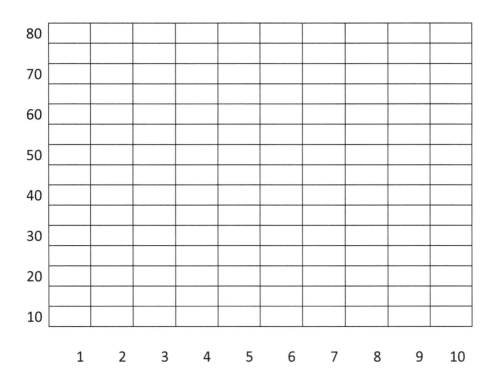

15-7 Probability Problems

1) A number is chosen at random from 1 to 10. Find the probability of selecting a 4 or smaller.

2) A number is chosen at random from 1 to 50. Find the probability of selecting multiples of 10.

3) A number is chosen at random from 1 to 10. Find the probability of selecting of 4 and factors of 6.

4) A number is chosen at random from 1 to 10. Find the probability of selecting a multiple of 3.

5) A number is chosen at random from 1 to 50. Find the probability of selecting prime numbers.

6) A number is chosen at random from 1 to 25. Find the probability of not selecting a composite number.

Answers of Worksheets – Chapter 15

15–1 Mean, Median, Mode, and Range of the Given Data

1) mean: 3, median: 2, mode: 2, range: 6
2) mean: 3.625, median: 3, mode: 2, range: 5
3) mean: 5.22, median: 4, mode: 4, range: 8
4) mean: 4, median: 4, mode: 4, range: 6
5) mean: 7, median: 7, mode: 5, 7, 8, range: 4
6) mean: 4.2, median: 4, mode: 1,2,4,5,9, range: 8
7) mean: 5, median: 5, mode: 5, range: 8
8) mean: 5.78, median: 6, mode: 7, range: 7
9) mean: 5, median: 5, mode: 2, 4, 5, 6, range: 7
10) mean: 6.125, median: 5, mode: 5, range: 8
11) mean: 3, median: 2, mode: 2, 5, range: 4
12) mean: 5, median: 5, mode: none, range: 7

15–2 Bar Graph

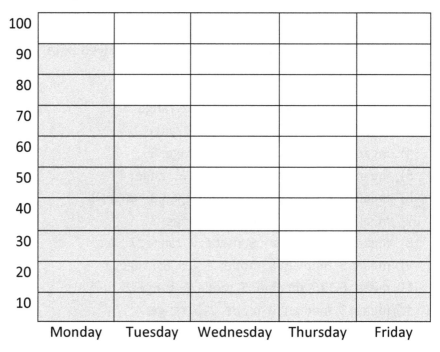

15–3 Box and Whisker Plots

1) 73, 84, 86, 95, 68, 67, 100, 94, 77, 80, 62, 79

Maximum: 100, Minimum: 62, Q_1: 70.5, Q_2: 79.5, Q_3: 90

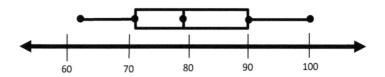

2) 11, 17, 22, 18, 23, 2, 3, 16, 21, 7, 8, 15, 5

Maximum: 23, Minimum: 2, Q_1: 6.5, Q_2: 15.5, Q_3: 19.5

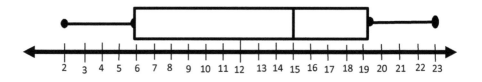

15–4 Stem–And–Leaf Plot

1)

Stem	leaf
7	2 4 9 9
8	3 6 8
9	1 5 7

key: 86

2)

Stem	leaf
1	9
2	6 6 6
3	3 7
4	8 8 9

key:

3)

Stem	leaf
4	1 2
5	3 4 4 8
6	5 5 7 9

key: 65

15–5 The Pie Graph or Circle Graph

1) red
2) 15%
3) black
4) 23%
5) 13%

15-6 Scatter Plots

X	Y
1	20
2	40
3	50
4	60

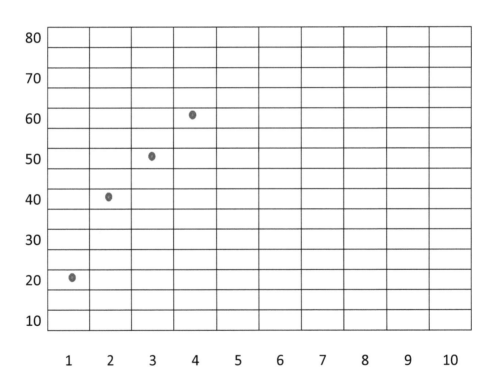

15−7 Probability Problems

1) $\dfrac{2}{5}$

2) $\dfrac{1}{10}$

3) $\dfrac{1}{2}$

4) $\dfrac{3}{10}$

5) $\dfrac{2}{510}$

6) $\dfrac{9}{25}$

ISEE Upper Level

Mathematics Achievement

Practice Test 1

- 47 questions
- Total time for this section: 40 Minutes
- Calculators are not allowed at the test.

ISEE Upper Level Math Workbook 2018

1) $\frac{7}{25}$ is equals to:

   a. 0.3

   b. 2.8

   c. 0.03

   d. 0.28

2) The sum of 8 numbers is greater than 240 and less than 320. Which of the following could be the average (arithmetic mean) of the numbers?

   a. 30

   b. 35

   c. 40

   d. 45

3) If $(4.2 + 4.3 + 4.5)\, x = x$, then what is the value of x?

   a. 0

   b. 1/10

   c. 1

   d. 10

4) Two dice are thrown simultaneously, what is the probability of getting a sum of 9 or 12?

   a. $\frac{1}{3}$

   b. $\frac{1}{4}$

   c. $\frac{1}{6}$

   d. $\frac{1}{12}$

5) Simplify $\dfrac{\frac{1}{2} - \frac{x+5}{4}}{\frac{x^2}{2} - \frac{5}{2}}$

   a. $\dfrac{3 - x}{x^2 - 10}$

   b. $\dfrac{3 - x}{2x^2 - 10}$

   c. $\dfrac{3 + x}{x^2 - 10}$

   d. $\dfrac{-3 - x}{2x^2 - 10}$

6) Find all values of x for which $4x^2 + 14x + 6 = 0$

   a. $-\frac{3}{2}, -\frac{1}{2}$

   b. $-\frac{1}{2}, -3$

   c. $-2, -\frac{1}{3}$

   d. $-\frac{2}{3}, \frac{1}{2}$

7) $(x + 7)(x + 5) =$

   a. $x^2 + 12x + 12$

   b. $2x + 12x + 12$

   c. $x^2 + 35x + 12$

   d. $x^2 + 12x + 35$

8) Which of the following graphs represents the compound inequality $-2 \leq 2x - 4 < 8$?

a.
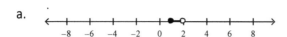

b.

c.

d.
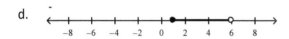

9) Solve.

$$|9 - (12 \div |2 - 5|)| = ?$$

a. 9

b. -6

c. 5

d. -5

10) $2 - 10 \div (4^2 \div 2) =$ ___

a. 6

b. $\dfrac{3}{4}$

c. -1

d. -2

11) Emily and Daniel have taken the same number of photos on their school trip. Emily has taken 5 times as many as photos as Claire and Daniel has taken 16 more photos than Claire. How many photos has Claire taken?

   a. 4

   b. 6

   c. 8

   d. 10

12) Emily lives 5 1/4 miles from where she works. When traveling to work, she walks to a bus stop 1/3 of the way to catch a bus. How many miles away from her house is the bus stop?

   a. 4 1/3 miles

   b. 4 3/4 miles

   c. 2 3/4 miles

   d. 1 3/4 miles

13) Use the diagram below to answer the question.

Given the lengths of the base and diagonal of the rectangle above, what is the length of height h, in terms of s?

a. $s\sqrt{6}$

b. $s\sqrt{7}$

c. $5s$

d. $5s^2$

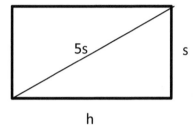

Use the chart below to answer the question.

Color	Number
White	20
Black	30
Beige	40

14) There are also purple marbles in the bag. Which of the following can NOT be the probability of randomly selecting a purple marble from the bag?

  a. $\frac{1}{10}$

  b. $\frac{1}{4}$

  c. $\frac{2}{5}$

  d. $\frac{7}{15}$

15) A square measures 6 inches on one side. By how much will the area be increased if its length is increased by 5 inches and its width decreased by 3 inches.

  a. 1 sq decreased

  b. 3 sq decreased

  c. 6 sq decreased

  d. 9 sq decreased

16) If a box contains red and blue balls in ratio of 2 : 3 red to blue, how many red balls are there if 90 blue balls are in the box?

   a. 40

   b. 60

   c. 80

   d. 30

17) How many 3 × 3 squares can fit inside a rectangle with a height of 54 and width of 12?

   a. 72

   b. 52

   c. 62

   d. 42

18) David makes a weekly salary of $220 plus 8% commission on his sales. What will his income be for a week in wich he makes sales totaling $1100.

   a. $328

   b. $318

   c. $308

   d. $298

19) $4x^2y^3 + 5x^3y^5 - (5x^2y^3 - 2x^3y^5) =$ ___

   a. $-x^2y^3$

   b. $6x^2y^3 - x^3y^5$

   c. $7x^2y^3$

   d. $7x^3y^5 - x^2y^3$

20) Given the diagram, what is the perimeter of the quadrilateral?

   a. 620

   b. 66

   c. 54

   d. 33,480

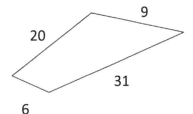

21) A mobile classroom is a rectangular block that is 50 feet by 10 feet in length and width respectively. If a student walks around the block once, how many yards does the student cover?

   a. 40 yards

   b. 35 yards

   c. 45 yards

   d. 30 yards

22) If a vehicle is driven 32 miles on Monday, 35 miles on Tuesday, and 29 miles on Wednesday, what is the average number of miles driven each day?

   a. 32 miles

   b. 31 miles

   c. 29 miles

   d. 33 miles

23) Find the area of a rectangle with a length of 138 feet and a width of 83 feet.

   a. 11, 504 sq. ft

   b. 11, 404 sq. ft

   c. 11,454 sq. ft

   d. 11, 204 sq. ft

24) $89 \div \frac{1}{8} = ?$

   a. 11.125

   b. 71

   c. 12

   d. 712

25) With an 22% discount, Ella was able to save $20.42 on a dress. What was the original price of the dress?

   a. $88.92

   b. $90.82

   c. $92.82

   d. $93.92

26) If a vehicle is driven 32 miles on Monday, 35 miles on Tuesday, and 29 miles on Wednesday, what is the average number of miles driven each day?

   a. 32 miles

   b. 31 miles

   c. 29 miles

   d. 33 miles

27) Solve for $2x^2 + 5 = 23$

   a. ± 4

   b. ± 9

   c. ± 10

   d. ± 3

28) A circle has a diameter of 16 inches. What is its approximate area?

   a. 200.96

   b. 100.48

   c. 64.00

   d. 12.56

29) If 6 garbage trucks can collect the trash of 36 homes in a day. How many trucks are needed to collect in 180 houses?

   a. 18

   b. 19

   c. 15

   d. 30

30) $56.78 \div 0.06 = ?$

   a. 94.633

   b. 946.33

   c. 9463.3

   d. 9.4633

Use the following table to answer question below.

DANIEL'S BIRD-WATCHING PROJECT	
DAY	NUMBER OF RAPTORS SEEN
Monday	?
Tuesday	9
Wednesday	14
Thursday	12
Friday	5
MEAN	10

31) This table shows the data Daniel collects while watching birds for one week. How many raptors did Daniel see on Monday?

   a. 10

   b. 11

   c. 12

   d. 13

32) A floppy disk shows 937,036 bytes free and 739,352 bytes used. If you delete a file of size 652,159 bytes and create a new file of size 599,986 bytes, how many free bytes will the floppy disk have?

   a. 687,179

   b. 791,525

   c. 884,867

   d. 989,209

33) 5 days 19 hours 35 minutes − 3 days 12 hours 22 minutes = ?

   a. 3 days 10 hours 13 minutes

   b. 2 days 7 hours 13 minutes

   c. 3 days 10 hours 13 minutes

   d. 2 days 7 hours 23 minutes

34) The base of a right triangle is 2 foot, and the interior angles are 45-45-90. What is its area?

   a. 2 foot squared

   b. 4 foot squared

   c. 3.5 feet squared

   d. 5.5 feet squared

35) Increased by 50%, the numbers 84 becomes:

   a. 42

   b. 100

   c. 126

   d. 130

36) Which equation represents the statement twice the difference between 6 times h and 3 gives 30.

a. $\frac{6h + 3}{2} = 30$

b. $6(2h + 3) = 30$

c. $2(6h + 3) = 30$

d. $3\frac{6h}{2} = 30$

37) A circle is inscribed in a square, as shown below.

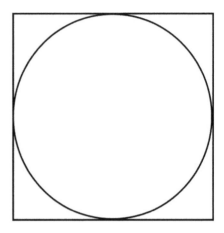

The area of the circle is 16π cm². What is the area of the square?

   a. 8 cm²

   b. 16 cm²

   c. 48 cm²

   d. 64 cm²

38) If $10 + x^{\frac{1}{2}} = 14$, then what is the value of $15 \times x$?

   a. 15

   b. 60

   c. 120

   d. 240

39) Triangle ABC is graphed on a coordinate grid with vertices at A (-3, -2), B (-1, 4) and C (7, 9). Triangle ABC is reflected over x axes to create triangle A'B'C'.

Which order pair represents the coordinate of C'?

   a. (7, 9)
   b. (-7, -9)
   c. (-7, 9)
   d. (7, -9)

40) Which set of ordered pairs represents y as a function of x?

   a. {(3, -2), (3, 7), (9, -8), (4, -7)}
   b. {(4, 2), (3, -9), (5, 8), (4, 7)}
   c. {(9, 12), (5, 7), (6, 11), (5, 18)}
   d. {(6, 1), (3, 1), (0, 5), (4, 5)}

41) How is this number written in scientific notation?

$$0.00002389$$

   a. 2.389×10^{-5}
   b. 23.89×10^{6}
   c. 0.2389×10^{-4}
   d. 2389×10^{-8}

42) Which graph shows a non-proportional linear relationship between x and y?

a.

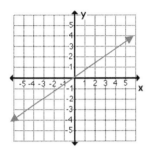

b.

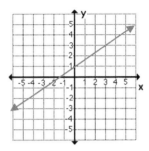

c.

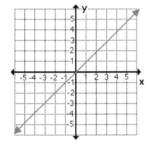

d.

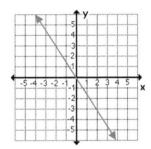

43) The rectangle on the coordinate grid is translated 5 units down and 4 units to the left.

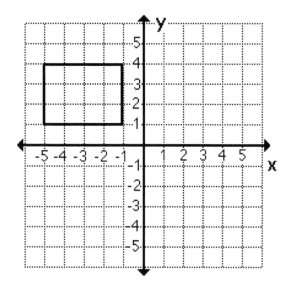

Which of the following describes this transformation?

a. $(x, y) \Rightarrow (x - 4, y + 5)$
b. $(x, y) \Rightarrow (x - 4, y - 5)$
c. $(x, y) \Rightarrow (x + 4, y + 5)$
d. $(x, y) \Rightarrow (x + 4, y - 5)$

44) A girl 160 cm tall, stands 360 cm from a lamp post at night. Her shadow from the light is 90 cm long. How high is the lamp post?

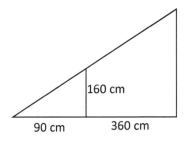

a. a. 240

b. b. 400

c. c. 600

d. d. 800

45) Which value of x makes the following inequality true?

$$\frac{3}{22} \leq x < 19\%$$

a. 0.13

b. $\frac{5}{36}$

c. $\sqrt{0.044}$

d. 0.124

46) The ratio of boys to girls in a school is 5:3. If there are 640 students in a school, how many boys are in the school?

   a. 240
   b. 360
   c. 400
   d. 540

47) The width of a box is one third of its length. The height of the box is one third of its width. If the length of the box is 27 cm, what is the volume of the box?

   a. 81 cm3
   b. 162 cm3
   c. 243 cm3
   d. 729 cm3

ISEE Upper Level

Mathematics Achievement

Practice Test 2

- 47 questions
- Total time for this section: 40 Minutes
- Calculators are not allowed at the test.

1) The drivers at G & G trucking must report the mileage on their trucks each week. The mileage reading of Ed's vehicle was 40,907 at the beginning of one week, and 41,053 at the end of the same week. What was the total number of miles driven by Ed that week?

   a. 46 miles

   b. 145 miles

   c. 146 miles

   d. 1,046 miles

2) Which equation represents the statement Three plus the sum of the squares of w and x is 32.

   a. 42

   b. $3(w^2 + x) = 32$

   c. 126

   d. 130

3) What is the solution of the following system of equations?
$$\begin{cases} -2x - y = -9 \\ 5x - 2y = 18 \end{cases}$$

   a. (-1, 2)

   b. (4, 1)

   c. (1, 4)

   d. (4, -2)

4) What is the area of an isosceles right triangle that has one leg that measures 6 cm?

    a. 18 cm

    b. 36 cm

    c. $6\sqrt{2}$ cm

    d. 72 cm

5) Which of the following is a factor of both $x^2 - 2x - 8$ and $x^2 - 6x + 8$?

    a. $(x - 4)$

    b. $(x + 4)$

    c. $(x - 2)$

    d. $(x + 2)$

6) $\frac{1}{6b^2} + \frac{1}{6b} = \frac{1}{b^2}$, then b = ?

    a. $-\frac{16}{15}$

    b. 5

    c. $-\frac{15}{16}$

    d. 8

7) $\frac{|3+x|}{7} \leq 5$, then x = ?

   a. $-38 \leq x \leq 35$

   b. $-38 \leq x \leq 32$

   c. $-32 \leq x \leq 38$

   d. $-32 \leq x \leq 32$

8) The cost, in thousand of dollars, of producing x thousands of textbooks is C (x) = x^2 + 10x + 30. The revenue, also in thousands of dollars, is R(x) = 4x. find the profit or loss if 3,000 textbooks are produced. (profit = revenue − cost)

   a. $21,000 loss

   b. $57,000 profit

   c. $3,000 profit

   d. $57,000 loss

9) Ella (E) is 4 years older than her friend Ava (A) who is 3 years younger than her sister Sofia (S). If E, A and S denote their ages, which one of the following represents the given information?

   a. $\begin{cases} E = A + 4 \\ S = A - 3 \end{cases}$

   b. $\begin{cases} E = A + 4 \\ A = S + 3 \end{cases}$

   c. $\begin{cases} A = E + 4 \\ S = A - 3 \end{cases}$

   d. $\begin{cases} E = A + 4 \\ A = S - 3 \end{cases}$

10) Which is the longest time?

   a. 23 hours

   b. 1520 minutes

   c. 2 days

   d. 4200 seconds

11) Write 523 in expanded form, using exponents.

   a. $(5 \times 10^3) + (2 \times 10^2) + (3 \times 10)$

   b. $(5 \times 10^2) + (2 \times 10^1) - 5$

   c. $(5 \times 10^2) + (2 \times 10^1) + 3$

   d. $(5 \times 10^1) + (2 \times 10^2) + 3$

12) A company pays its writer $4 for every 400 words written. How much will a writer earn for an article with 960 words?

   a. $11

   b. $5.6

   c. $9.6

   d. $8.7

13) A circular logo is enlarged to fit the lid of a jar. The new diameter is 60% larger than the original. By what percentage has the area of the logo increased?

   a. 40%

   b. 30%

   c. 60%

   d. 20%

14) A circle has a diameter of 8 inches. What is its approximate circumference?

   a. 6.28

   b. 25.12

   c. 34.85

   d. 35.12

15) How many square feet of tile is needed for a 18 foot x 18 foot room?

    a. 72 square feet

    b. 108 square feet

    c. 324 square feet

    d. 216 square feet

16) $(3x + 3)(x + 5)$

    a. $4x + 8$

    b. $3x + 3x + 15$

    c. $3x^2 + 18x + 15$

    d. $3x^2 + 3$

17) A scoutmaster is preparing his troop for their annual fishing expedition. He surveys each of his scouts to find out how many fishing poles they own.

Fishing Poles Owned	
# of Fishing Poles	Number of Scouts Owning This Number
0	12
1	8
2	4
3	7
4	13
5	9

a. 4

b. 5

c. 2

d. 0

ISEE Upper Level Math Workbook 2018

18) David's motorcycle stalled at the beach and he called the towing company. They charged him $ 3.45 per mile for the first 22 miles and then $4.25 per mile for each mile over 22. David was 26 miles from the motorcycle repair shop. How much was David's towing bill?

   a. $84.4

   b. $71.9

   c. $90.9

   d. $92.9

19) You work in a hospital and make $17.20 per hour for a 40 hour a week. If you work the night shift you get a slight differential added at $3.25 per hour worked during this shift. You just completed your first week and worked 25 hours on a regular shift and 5 hours on the night shift. What is the total amount you earned this week?

   a. $527.9

   b. $519.58

   c. $533.5

   d. $523.58

20) If x is 45% percent of 820, what is x?

   a. 185

   b. 369

   c. 402

   d. 720

21) What is the area of an isosceles right triangle that has one leg that measures 4 cm?

   a. 18 cm

   b. 36 cm

   c. $6\sqrt{2}$ cm

   d. 72 cm

22) What's the area of the rectangle with the black border?

   a. 192

   b. 28

   c. 40

   d. 42

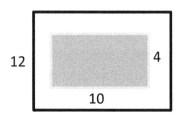

23) 79.22 ÷ 0.05 = ?

   a. 15.844

   b. 1,584.4

   c. 1,58.44

   d. 1.5844

24) A bread recipe calls for $3\frac{1}{3}$ cups of flour. If you only have $2\frac{5}{6}$ cups, how much more flour is needed?

   a. 1

   b. $\frac{1}{2}$

   c. 2

   d. $\frac{7}{6}$

25) The equation of a line is given as : y = 5 x – 3. Which of the following points does not lie on the line?

   a. (1, 2)

   b. (–2, –13)

   c. (3, 18)

   d. (2, 7)

26) $\frac{13}{25}$ is equal to:

   a. 5.2

   b. 0.52

   c. 0.05

   d. 0.5

27) If $x + y$ = 12, what is the value of $8x + 8y$?

   a. 192

   b. 48

   c. 104

   d. 96

28) $\dfrac{\begin{array}{r}37\ \text{hr.}\ \ 25\ \text{min.}\\ 23\ \text{hr.}\ \ 38\ \text{min.}\end{array}}{\ }$

   a. 12 hr. 57 min.

   b. 12 hr. 47 min.

   c. 13 hr. 47 min.

   d. 13 hr. 57 min.

29) A car uses 15 gallons of gas to travel 450 miles. How many miles per gallon does the car get?

a. 28 miles per gallon

b. 32 miles per gallon

c. 30 miles per gallon

d. 34 miles per gallon

30) Find the perimeter of a rectangle with the dimensions 89 × 55.

a. 4,895

b. 288

c. 144

d. 134

31) What's the reciprocal of $\frac{x^3}{16}$?

a. $\frac{16}{x^3} - 1$

b. $\frac{48}{x^3}$

c. $\frac{16}{x^3} + 1$

d. $\frac{16}{x^3}$

32) Mario loaned Jett $1200 at a yearly interest rate of 5%. After one year what is the interest owned on this loan?

   a. $126

   b. $60

   c. $5

   d. $1260

33) Ellis just got hired for on-the-road sales and will travel about 2,500 miles a week during a 80 hour work week. If the time spent raveling is $\frac{3}{5}$ of his week, how many hours a week will he be on the road?

   a. Ellis spends about 34 hours of his 80 hour work week on the road.

   b. Ellis spends about 48 hours of his 80 hour work week on the road.

   c. Ellis spends about 43 hours of his 80 hour work week on the road.

   d. Ellis spends about 40 hours of his 80 hour work week on the road.

34) Given that x = 0.6 and y = 6, what is the value of $2x^2(y + 4)$?

   a. 7.2

   b. 8.2

   c. 11.2

   d. 13.2

35) Karen is 9 years older than her sister Michelle, and Michelle is 4 years younger than her brother David. If the sum of their ages is 82, how old is Michelle?

    a. 21

    b. 25

    c. 29

    d. 23

36) Calculate the area of a parallelogram with a base of 2 feet and height of 2.4 feet.

    a. 2.8 square feet

    b. 4.2 square feet

    c. 4.8 square feet

    d. 4.0 square feet

37) A shirt costing $200 is discounted 15%. After a month, the shirt is discounted another 15%. Which of the following expressions can be used to find the selling price of the shirt?

    a. (200) (0.70)
    b. (200) − 200 (0.30)
    c. (200) (0.15) − (200) (0.15)
    d. (200) (0.85) (0.85)

38) In a school, the ratio of number of boys to girls is 3:7. If the number of boys is 180, what is the total number of students in the school?

   a. 390
   b. 500
   c. 540
   d. 600

39) A tree 32 feet tall casts a shadow 12 feet long. Jack is 6 feet tall. How long is Jack's shadow?

   a. 2.25 ft
   b. 4 ft
   c. 4.25 ft
   d. 8 ft

40) What is the area of the shaded region if the diameter of the bigger circle is 12 inches and the diameter of the smaller circle is 8 inches.

a. 16 π inch²
b. 20 π inch²
c. 36 π inch²
d. 80 π inch²

41) 5 less than twice a positive integer is 83. What is the integer?

a. 39
b. 41
c. 42
d. 44

42) Which of the following points lies on the line $4x + 6y = 14$?

a. (2, 1)
b. (-1, 3)
c. (-3, 4)
d. (2, 2)

43) An angle is equal to one fifth of its supplement. What is the measure of that angle?

    a. 20
    b. 30
    c. 45
    d. 60

44) 1.2 is what percent of 24?

    a. 1.2
    b. 5
    c. 12
    d. 24

45) Right triangle ABC has two legs of lengths 6 cm (AB) and 8 cm (AC). What is the length of the third side (BC)?

    a. 4 cm
    b. 6 cm
    c. 8 cm
    d. 10 cm

46) Simplify $6x^2y^3(2x^2y)^3 =$

    a. $12x^4y^6$
    b. $12x^8y^6$
    c. $48x^4y^6$
    A. $48x^8y^6$

47) What is the result of the expression

$$\begin{vmatrix} 3 & 6 \\ -1 & -3 \\ -5 & -1 \end{vmatrix} + \begin{vmatrix} 0 & -1 \\ 6 & 0 \\ 2 & 3 \end{vmatrix} ?$$

a. $\begin{vmatrix} 0 & -1 \\ 6 & 0 \\ 2 & 3 \end{vmatrix}$

b. $\begin{vmatrix} 3 & 6 \\ -1 & -3 \\ -5 & -1 \end{vmatrix}$

c. $\begin{vmatrix} 3 & 5 \\ 5 & -3 \\ -3 & 2 \end{vmatrix}$

d. $\begin{vmatrix} 0 & -3 \\ -6 & 0 \\ -10 & -3 \end{vmatrix}$

ISEE Upper Level Tests

Answer Keys

Practice Test 1

1)	d	16)	b	31)	a	46)	c
2)	b	17)	a	32)	d	47)	d
3)	a	18)	c	33)	b		
4)	d	19)	d	34)	a		
5)	d	20)	b	35)	c		
6)	b	21)	a	36)	c		
7)	d	22)	a	37)	d		
8)	d	23)	c	38)	d		
9)	a	24)	d	39)	d		
10)	c	25)	c	40)	d		
11)	a	26)	a	41)	a		
12)	d	27)	d	42)	b		
13)	a	28)	a	43)	b		
14)	d	29)	d	44)	d		
15)	b	30)	b	45)	b		

Practice Test 2								
1)	c	16)	c	31)	d	46)	d
2)	b	17)	a	32)	d	47)	c
3)	b	18)	d	33)	d		
4)	a	19)	c	34)	a		
5)	a	20)	b	35)	d		
6)	b	21)	a	36)	c		
7)	b	22)	a	37)	d		
8)	d	23)	b	38)	d		
9)	d	24)	b	39)	a		
10)	c	25)	c	40)	b		
11)	c	26)	b	41)	d		
12)	c	27)	d	42)	a		
13)	b	28)	c	43)	b		
14)	a	29)	c	44)	b		
15)	a	30)	b	45)	d		

"Effortless Math" Publications

Effortless Math authors' team strives to prepare and publish the best quality Mathematics learning resources to make learning Math easier for all. We hope that our publications help you or your student learn Math in an effective way.

We all in Effortless Math wish you good luck and successful studies!

Effortless Math Authors

Online Math Lessons

Enjoy interactive Math lessons online
with the best Math teachers

Online Math learning that's effective, affordable, flexible, and fun

Learn Math wherever you want; when you want
Ultimate flexibility. You can now learn Math online, enjoy high quality engaging lessons no matter where in the world you are. It's affordable too.

Learn Math with one-on-one classes
We provide one-on-one Math tutoring online. We believe that one-to-one tutoring is the most effective way to learn Math.

Qualified Math tutors
Working with the best Math tutors in the world is the key to success! Our tutors give you the support and motivation you need to succeed with a personal touch.

Online Math Lessons

It's easy! Here's how it works.

1- Request a FREE introductory session.

2- Meet a Math tutor online.

3- Start Learning Math in Minutes.

Send Email to: info@EffortlessMath.com

CPSIA information can be obtained
at www.ICGtesting.com
Printed in the USA
LVHW111910241121
704372LV00011B/657